T0337425

FROM THE FOX SERIES

SLEEPY HOLLOW

CREATING HEROES, DEMONS & MONSTERS

Tara Bennett
Paul Terry

TITAN BOOKS

SleepyHollow: Creating Heroes, Demons and Monsters
ISBN: 9781783298372

Published by
Titan Books
A division of Titan Publishing Group Ltd.
144 Southwark St, London. SE1 0UP

www.TitanBooks.com

First edition: November 2015

10 9 8 7 6 5 4 3 2 1

Photo page 4 courtesy of Aaron Baiers.

Below: *Ichabod hides from the Headless Horseman in 'Magnum Opus.'*

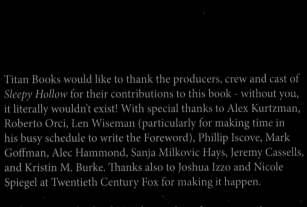

Titan Books would like to thank the producers, crew and cast of
Sleepy Hollow for their contributions to this book - without you,
it literally wouldn't exist! With special thanks to Alex Kurtzman,
Roberto Orci, Len Wiseman (particularly for making time in
his busy schedule to write the Foreword), Phillip Iscove, Mark
Goffman, Alec Hammond, Sanja Milkovic Hays, Jeremy Cassells,
and Kristin M. Burke. Thanks also to Joshua Izzo and Nicole
Spiegel at Twentieth Century Fox for making it happen.

Did you enjoy this book? We love to hear from our readers.
Please e-mail us at: readerfeedback@titanemail.com or write to
Reader Feedback at the above address.

To receive advance information, news, competitions, and
exclusive offers online, please sign up for the Titan newsletter on
our website: www.titanbooks.com

A CIP catalogue record for this title is available from the
British Library.

Printed and bound in U.S.A..

Contents

Foreword

I've always been drawn to projects that present an opportunity for creative world building and what better show to do that with than *Sleepy Hollow*. From the first moment I heard the idea with the other producers I instantly fell in love with the project and the potential to create something so exciting on a large canvas with endless possibilities. It's been an amazing experience to work on such an inventive series with the rest of our talented team. Creating the design and vision of the show has been one of the most exciting parts and so we wanted our fans to join in the experience by sharing a special look at the design of the show and how we bring *Sleepy Hollow* to life.

At the earliest stages of development one of the first things we did was begin envisioning what the Headless Horseman would look like. We obviously wanted to make him terrifying, but we also wanted to make him look cool – *really cool*. We started playing with different ideas of how to update this iconic villain and introduce him to the present day with a supernatural twist. Once we had his look nailed down (original concept art pictured opposite) we knew the sky was the limit and we didn't hold back there.

One of the most unique things about the show that I love is the blend of so many different and rich elements. From the Headless Horseman and our "twistory" moments, to our weekly creatures, and most importantly, our heroes. Every story and every character presents a new challenge and a new opportunity to create something special and bring it to life. From top to bottom, we have such a talented team in place across all departments that help make this happen and carve out our own voice for the show. It truly would not be possible to make this show without our amazing team who put everything they have into it.

Our goal has always been to make each episode feel like a movie so our fans can have a cinematic experience on their television every single week. We do believe that is one of the promises of the show that make it unique and it's what our fans have come to expect – after all, we do it for all you passionate Sleepyheads out there. So we invite you to continue on this journey with us and take a peek behind the curtain of the magical and haunting world that is *Sleepy Hollow*.

Don't Lose Your Head,

Len Wiseman
Executive Producer

Below: *Behind-the-scenes shooting a night-time graveyard scene for the pilot.*

The Legend of Sleepy Hollow

To say that there's nothing on television quite like *Sleepy Hollow* really isn't just flagrant hyperbole. It's the truth. What other show can boast DNA comprised of such disparate parts as mythological mysteries, historical fiction, chilling horror, sociological meditations, genuine wit, as well as being both a period *and* a contemporary piece?

Sleepy Hollow is a television series that has defied easy labels since it debuted. From the pilot episode where Ichabod Crane, Washington Irving's classic literary character, was reawakened in our contemporary world, the series has gleefully reveled in surprising audiences as an audacious, genre-busting mash-up that makes weaving a high-concept premise into incredibly relatable characters look effortless.

The creation of writers Alex Kurtzman, Roberto Orci, Phillip Iscove, and director Len Wiseman, *Sleepy Hollow* burst onto the television landscape in September 2013 from a premise that evolved extensively from its inception to execution. Executive producer and co-creator Alex Kurtzman reveals that the kernel of the idea for the show stemmed from his initial interest in creating a series around one particular subject: witches.

"I had been thinking that it seemed like such an interesting time period with amazing mythologies," Kurtzman recalls. "It felt like ripe territory." From there, Kurtzman and Orci worked on that concept while taking meetings with writers regarding other properties that their production company, K/O Paperworks, might develop. "[Writer] Phil Iscove came in and said he'd love to do a show about the town of Sleepy Hollow, but he wasn't interested in doing it [as a] period piece because it had been done before." Iscove really ignited the light bulb of inspiration as he suggested doing the Washington Irving story set in modern day.

Kurtzman continues, "That idea grew mostly because it seemed like an opportunity to tap into my all-time favorite show in the history of television, *Twin Peaks*. Growing up, I was obsessed with that show. It hugely influenced me on so many different levels. The idea of getting to tell a story about a small town and the strange things going on underneath its surface, yet in a way that leaned even harder into the horror genre, was really exciting to all of us."

The writers then honed their focus on the character of Ichabod Crane, who would remain a protagonist in their reworking. "The idea of a fish out of water story – a man from the past who comes to present day – was a delicious idea," Kurtzman explains. "It's also a very tricky one in that there were many terrible versions of that idea. All of the expected gags of a man from 1776 coming to our time now could be hokey. Therefore we spent a lot of time giving a ton of thought to how we could make our Ichabod a very interesting lens through which our modern culture is observed, with wit and humor, as opposed to hokiness. It started as, 'Maybe he's very quiet with his observing?' but then suddenly we were milking the opportunity of having an observer in our world. As his character started to grow, given that we were paying homage to the short story but also were reinventing quite a bit of the mythology, it struck us that it might be very interesting if Crane were British. He could have actually fought for the British during the war. Then, because of events we come to learn over the course of the series, he defected and became an American. He's a double foreigner in two very strange worlds: first in his own time period, but then ours. Suddenly," Kurtzman says with a smile, "Crane and his voice came alive when he was British."

Knowing that Crane would need a foil to guide him through our world, the creative team settled on a local cop in Tarrytown whom they named Abigail 'Abbie' Mills. The team liked the idea of a modern woman ushering a retro man into contemporary society, but they were also very wary of the dynamic of a male/female investigative team coming across as derivative. Kurtzman explains, "The funny thing with Abbie was that those two could have easily fallen into a Mulder/Scully [from *The X-Files*] paradigm, another one of our favorite shows that we have tipped quite a bit of our hat to on *Sleepy*. The problem was that [dynamic] had been done so well, so we wanted to do something original, while also recognizing the heritage that we were drawing from. We didn't want to just make her the skeptic who was constantly saying to Ichabod, 'I don't believe it. I don't know why.' What eventually broke through for us with Abbie was that her story needed to be more insane than Crane's," Kurtzman laughs. "We came up with the idea that Abbie had a childhood in which she had encountered a literal demon, had repressed it since then, and has been doing everything possible to run away both from the town and from her experience. The arrival of this stranger, Crane, into the town in the pilot, just when she is thinking about leaving, was going to be the catalyst to force her to deal with things. Her literal inner demons became outer demons. That became wildly interesting to us. It felt like it was a different kind of believer/skeptic dynamic and that we were doing something original."

With a setting and the two protagonists settled, the creative team then brought Mark Goffman into the creative fold as the show's executive producer/showrunner. Together they turned their attention to figuring out the tone of *Sleepy Hollow*, which they all agreed needed to be bold. "I think once we understood what the actual emotional reality was for the characters, we took huge leaps from there," Kurtzman says of their ideas for the creative boundaries of the series. "Without having a credible and believable reason for these characters to exist in our story, and without understanding how they were emotionally reacting to the insanity that was before them, we wouldn't have been able to then go, 'Okay, we have such a solid base here, we should go crazy and really push it.'"

"We wanted the show to be a *fun* fan experience," Mark Goffman emphasizes. "Everything started from the perspective of what would be fun within all of these genres? We often describe the show as this enormous mash-up of tones and colors. What also became so fun was asking, 'How wild and crazy can we go?' We decided there would always be a cliff's edge that we'd forever be walking along in terms of pushing things to the very edge and almost falling off. Alex Kurtzman would always say, 'We're microns away from falling off,'" Goffman chuckles. "That was the overriding philosophy we began with."

The key to not falling off the cliff became the idea that Ichabod and Abbie would anchor whatever fantastical stories, demons and mythology the writers could throw at them. "What attracted me to do the show," Goffman states, "was the grounded reality in which these characters existed. That had to be ingrained in the fabric of the show – that it didn't feel like a comic book or graphic novel or a surreal/hyper-real environment. It always had to feel real."

Aesthetics

With "wild and crazy" as their creative mantra, the *Sleepy Hollow* creative core looked to one particular member of their team to guide them in establishing the eventual signature look of the show. "Len Wiseman really developed the visual aesthetic of the show," Alex Kurtzman says with admiration for their co-creator. "He was so responsible for building the world. Len's never had an idea we've disagreed with. That's a weird thing to say, but it's true. We have this instant ability to understand each other's visions. He brought an amazing, creepy, strange vibe to the tone of the show that is hugely his contribution."

Well-known for creating the visually dazzling *Underworld* film franchise, Wiseman freely admits he is a connoisseur of all things monsters and demons. With *Sleepy Hollow* – his first foray into genre television creation – Wiseman wanted to bring a feature production-rich aesthetic to the small screen. "I am really trying to present things that have not been seen, or that are a twist on what [audiences] have seen before," Wiseman says of his visual intentions for the series. "It is very easy with the creature aspect, or the supernatural aspect, to just go to the stock direction you have seen before with supernatural shows. I really wanted to make a point with *Sleepy Hollow* that you can have a bit of a cinematic experience every week."

From the pilot, Wiseman helped assemble a team of top-notch artisans from the worlds of film and television to come together and make *Sleepy Hollow* stand out from the episodic pack. "We have such a stellar production team for a lot of reasons but mostly because we make a movie every week," Kurtzman says of the show's various production departments. "To have a show with this many visual effects, and this much action, horror and quiet emotional scenes is incredibly challenging on the crew. It's a very, very hard thing to do but they do it with incredible dedication and care because they're proud of the work they're creating, and the world we've all built. We've had the very good fortune of having some amazing creature designers and some brilliant directors realize this vision. The word gratitude comes up because these kinds of shows are very difficult to sustain. To get these talented people to help us continue the vision is truly extraordinary."

For the pilot, the original visual team included production designer Alec Hammond (*Southland Tales*, *RED*), director of photography Kramer Morgenthau (*Thor: The Dark World*), costume designer Sanja Milkovic Hays (the *Fast and Furious* films), makeup department head Leo Corey Castellano (*Creed*), and visual effects supervisor Jason Michael Zimmerman (*Community*, *Fringe*). It was their cumulative efforts that established the look of the series and how it would proceed over two seasons, with various other creative department heads and collaborators. But from the start, their creative core was one particular image.

"The initial conversations about *Sleepy Hollow*'s aesthetics, and really what its look was based on, came from a single image that Len had done for the show: a Redcoat, a Revolutionary War soldier, without a head... carrying a machine gun," original production designer Alec Hammond says with a smile. "When I first sat down with him to talk about the script and the world, he showed me that. It became the jumping-off point. The series really needed to have scares, thrills, and have the production values and qualities of a major feature, even if we were doing it on a weekly basis."

"From the beginning, like any creative process, it's a collaboration," original costume designer Sanja Milkovic Hays remembers about the early days of the series. "Len Wiseman was the director of the pilot, and he is extremely visual. He knows what he wants. We talked about not making *Sleepy Hollow* strictly a period show, but bringing the story to a whole new audience. We wanted to make it a little bit more of a mixture, and in a sense, a modern version of the period. It's a fantasy show, so you can't stick strictly to the history books anyway. With the Revolutionary War and the costumes, we were staying pretty close to that, but when it came to the fantasy characters and elements, that was a different situation to deal with.

"I'm really proud that my colleagues and I were able to establish the look of the show in such a short space of time," she continues. "That's a big credit to Len and his guidance that we managed to make everything look real. It was probably one of the most difficult things I've ever done."

It's through their work to achieve such creative excellence, as reflected in the pages that follow, that audiences have embraced a series that is almost impossible to explain in a short, coherent sentence. The visuals supersede the need for an easy logline, as evidenced in captivated audiences who are never quite sure what they're going to see week after week. "I think we're most proud of how quickly people embraced the show, were willing to go on the ride, and to accept the reality of the world we were building, really without question," Kurtzman says of *Sleepy Hollow*'s adventurous audience. "It was interesting to us, because for very good reasons, when people were first seeing the trailers, and conceptually thinking about a show like this, they were like, 'This sounds like the worst show *ever*! What a weird mish-mash of tones. What is it?!' To our absolute delight, when we premiered the pilot – across the board – the response was, 'This isn't what we expected at all. It's a lot better!'"

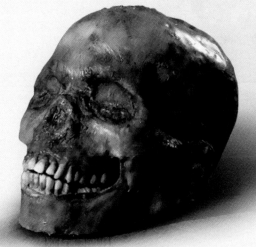

Previous Page: *One of the Headless Horseman's skull props.*

This Spread: *Early concept art for the Headless Horseman.*

The Darkest Depths of Sleepy Hollow

While *Sleepy Hollow* may be crafted around a mélange of genres and tones, its heart beats to the drum of horror. From the beginning, executive producer Len Wiseman's mandate has been to craft a television show that feels like the [horror] movies the creators grew up with. In practice, that means *Sleepy Hollow* is a production that revolves around original, practical creations of makeup, design, prosthetics, and costuming, with augmenting visual effects.

In the writers' room, executive producer Mark Goffman says it's always been about creating a balance between giving their audiences genuine frights, and then tempering that with humor that allows the intensity of their creatures and demons to be modulated. "I don't think we ever felt, 'Let's not do that because it's too scary,'" Goffman says of their demon development. "If we could create a creature that was incredibly scary, that was the goal. Some episodes are slightly scarier than others, some are slightly funnier, and some have both qualities. As we're crafting the season, we want to have episodes that feel different. But when we're crafting something scary, we want to craft the scariest version.

"Gory is another aspect," he continues. "We aren't going for shock value or gore or disgust. We remember that nine and ten year olds seem to be watching as well, and families tell us they are watching it together. So it's not about grossing people out. The horror has to be part of the story we are telling; that's the primary directive."

Characters and Creatures

The men responsible for every *Sleepy Hollow* demon that's graced screens to date are Len Wiseman and makeup department head Corey Castellano. "[To make this show], it takes somebody who has passion and Corey is incredibly talented," Wiseman says of Castellano. "We also share a very similar aesthetic for creatures and design and what we're trying to pull off."

From his twenty-plus years as a makeup artist, Castellano brought to *Sleepy Hollow* his own adoration for design and creation of otherworldly creatures. It's rare for a series to require the sheer amount of new creatures featured in *Sleepy Hollow* in the time television production demands, which Castellano says is what attracted him to the project.

"On this show, there is a freedom to develop a design aesthetic for all of these creatures," he explains. "It was kind of wide open, even though they were things that were rooted in known myths, or ideas that have been kicked around for centuries. Everybody was really on board for trying to push things in a fresh direction. And for the period work, we did strive to retain at least some semblance of things in a correct nature, which Kristin [Burke] was amazing at as far as the costuming went. We did what we could as far as the constraints we had regarding hair and makeup."

For Wiseman, working with Castellano and the production team has been an eye-opening experience in speed designing and development. "I will say it is very different from television to

features," Wiseman says with a light laugh. "You just don't have the time and the money. In the feature world, you can design a whole creature, sculpt it and put it together, and if it doesn't really work, you go back and you start again and you refine and refine. Well, we don't have time. Often when we see the final product of a creature it's the day that it is shooting that it is really done and we can really take a look at it."

In order to be ready for set, Wiseman says their creative circle has created a process. "Corey will put together a lot of reference. I will often do sketches." All of that is in preparation for a creative meeting that includes executive producer Mark Goffman. "At least once a month – and probably a little more regularly than that, especially at the beginning of a season – we have creature meetings," says Goffman. "We'll all video conference in with a feed from Wilmington to the writers' offices, and Len will usually be on speaker as well. We'll all be on our computers and looking at images. Corey will sketch something and then Len will sketch something, and we'll take a look at it and comment on it. To make the show feel as authentic and as tangible as possible, we like our creatures to be practical, so we really have in-depth discussions. It takes months."

Wiseman continues, "I am on the phone with them and I'm doing doodles and sketches and I take a picture and text them pictures as we are on the call. That is often how we do it and that is how fast we have to do it. There are many times I'm on the computer, whether it is drawing up stuff or looking at references, at 4 o'clock in the morning because there's a part of me that just is drawn to it and I love it. It is fun to be able to create these creatures!"

Once a rough character design is in place, Goffman says, "Then we need to know, 'What is that character going to be doing in the script?' And that is something that, yet again, we spend a lot of time on. Myself and the writer will be in constant communication with Corey, our producer, and the VFX team and Len. We all go back and forth, looking at the possibilities of what can we do that will service, first and foremost, the story, but also what would be cool and really give us the moments we want. We are very fortunate to have a pretty healthy budget to do things right on this show. We always have the philosophy of, 'Well, we're gonna do it right, or we'll find another way.' There is a very high bar in terms of all the sequences. They have to look realistic, or we will change the sequence."

The result is a pantheon of demons that have horrified and delighted audiences. Intricate, clever, and haunting, the creatures of *Sleepy Hollow* are the culmination of creative minds and technicians working in accelerated harmony. "I'm proud of everything that we've done," Castellano says of their rogues gallery. "I have such a great team with me that we are able to maintain a really great level of work throughout. On a lot of shows, you see that they start strong and either time, energy, or budget reduces that. People lose track and sometimes recycle or reuse [prosthetic] pieces they've made. That's something that we never wanted to do. We've always tried to push the boundaries and achieve a level of work that we could all walk away from feeling proud of. I think we do that."

'Len Wiseman, Mark Goffman and everybody have to pitch ideas and decide on what the best approach is for any Horseman. Will it be fully practical? Will we ever see a human being tied into it? Should it always be an animated suit of armor? The furthest we got on Pestilence was to establish the basic look of the suit of armor. Then it was a matter of, 'Are we ever going to see its face? If so, what should we see?' It's a really involved process.'

Corey Castellano (Makeup Department Head)

While the narrative of *Sleepy Hollow* places the series in upstate New York, in actuality the series has always been shot 622 miles south in the state of North Carolina. Through the magic of production design, and the skills of the art department, property masters, location scouts and individual set-making craftsmen, *Sleepy Hollow* has always looked authentic to its geography and the historical eras featured in its storytelling.

In the early days of developing the look of the show's version of Sleepy Hollow, Mark Goffman remembers that they wanted to achieve the "retro feel" of small-town America. "We wanted Ichabod Crane, who is this founder of America, to exist in something that's relatable to him and not hi-tech. So very early on we made a conscious decision not to go with sleek styles, metals, and shiny new tones. A lot of the props and the production design that we would go over, we wanted them to either have a Colonial era feel or something that had been in the Colonial era that is still around today. That way it had been built upon from a foundation of America, as opposed to being wholly new."

"Although we never shot anything there, Sleepy Hollow is a wonderful idea of a place," pilot production designer Alec Hammond explains. "You have a small town right on the Hudson River outside of New York. You're removed from everything. You're literally a sleepy little village. But, as soon as you scrape the ground, a million things are uncovered," he says with devilish intent.

"With this show, they're uncovered both in the supernatural and in the historical. In some ways, we use that idea both with literal underground worlds," he continues. "In 'Blood Moon,' we reveal this labyrinth of tunnels underneath Sleepy Hollow where you see a witch, and things that look like they shouldn't ever be able to exist in the physical places they do. Ichabod crawls out of a hole underneath a damn… with an entire cave underneath. I grew up in a small town, and we tried to tap into the kind of mystery that's underneath any small town, where you think there could be so much more there. The 'so much more than there is' is both the entire history of the founding of the United States and also lots and lots of monsters."

For the pilot episode, it was decided Charlotte, North Carolina would be the home base for the initial production. "In looking for where to set the series, we felt it was extremely important to keep this 'small town' feel and be able to shoot locations," Goffman explains. "It was not going be a show that was shot in front of greenscreen on

a sound stage. That would not lend itself to the look and feel that we were trying to establish."

While Charlotte offered the needed production services and personnel to make the pilot episode, Hammond remembers the city itself was a challenge in terms of finding era-appropriate locales. "Charlotte didn't even have 10,000 people in it until the 19th century," he explains. "Everything was dated past any time that we were doing flashbacks, so there was zero real Colonial architecture. It didn't reach 100,000 people until decades later. But we were able to do this tour outside of Charlotte and snag all these little towns that were within our shooting radius. There were some areas that seemed to have the right mix of stuff that felt Colonial, *was* Colonial, and then things that had been built more recently. As long as our Sleepy Hollow had that mixture, then it seemed like the right kind of place. We didn't want somewhere that was completely new. We wanted somewhere that really had that merge of old and new."

After *Sleepy Hollow* was picked up to series, the production moved to Screen Gems Studios in Wilmington, North Carolina, where they could build permanent sets, such as The Archives and Mabie's Tavern, and use the wooded grounds for various locations throughout the first two seasons. "Wilmington offered a mix of things that were still around from the Colonial era," Goffman explains. "It also still has a small-town feel because it literally is a small town."

"It was a great place to be in and had a great set of personnel there," second season production designer Jeremy Cassells says of their home. "The [construction team] were all classically trained (in New York) plasterers. They had a great skill set that we drew upon, because there weren't that many locations downtown that we could really use."

The town of New Bern also became a key location for several important locations, including the exterior of Ichabod Crane's home and the streets leading to Ben Franklin's abode, among others. "We wanted to find somewhere we could go to for a week or two weeks, and then come back three months later and be able to have as our home base as an actual preserved Colonial village and town," Hammond says of their use of New Bern. "We did the witch burning there, and they went back a number of times in that first season. New Bern was actually the Colonial head of government in North Carolina for a moment. There is a whole section of town that actually dates to the correct period, and it's preserved."

'We designed an entire Colonial backlot for the series, of 27 buildings, but didn't get to build much of it. I was immensely proud of being able to design that with everybody who worked on it. Then we found New Bern and built some, but not all of it. I thought that the permanent sets that we were left with were really good. I didn't get bored of them!'

Alec Hammond (Original Production Designer)

J.J. STONER PUBLISHER, MADISON, WIS.

NEW CASTLE
1. LINCOLN ACADEMY
2. DISTRICT SCHOOL
3. R.R. DEPOT
4. FIRE ENGINE HOUSE
5. CUNGREGATIONAL } CHURCH
6. EPISCOPAL
7. CEMETERY

BIRDS EYE

SLEEPY HOLL

LINCOLN HALL

A. RÜGER DEL

OF THE VILLAGES OF

NEW YORK

Ichabod Crane

Unlike the gangly pedagogue described in Washington Irving's writing, *Sleepy Hollow's* Ichabod Crane, as embodied by actor Tom Mison, cuts a handsome figure as well as possessing a keen intellect. In broadening the scope of the character, the creators gave former Oxford professor Ichabod a military career, first for the British, and then as a spy for the Colonial Army. As a soldier, Crane would possess a more complex backstory that would tie into the mythology of the Headless Horseman, as well as put him in the confidence of some of America's earliest heads of state.

Thus the Ichabod Crane of this adaptation needed to look commanding, scholarly, yet subtly heroic. So makeup department head Corey Castellano developed a look to reflect the show's more robust take on the character. "We did deviate from the original Washington Irving story in that he was a schoolteacher afraid of everything," Castellano explains. "Our Crane is a rugged guy, a revolutionary, so we were trying to

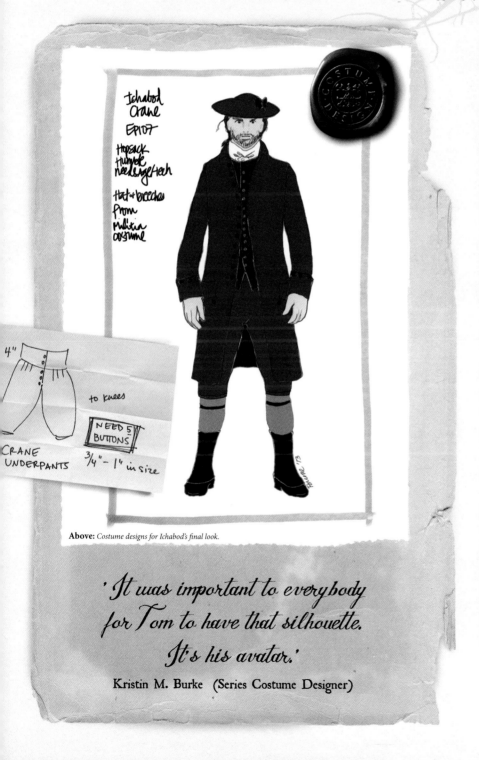

Above: *Costume designs for Ichabod's final look.*

'It was important to everybody for Tom to have that silhouette. It's his avatar.'

Kristin M. Burke (Series Costume Designer)

Opposite and Above: *Initial concepts for Ichabod Crane showing layers of a costume, with a different contemporary coat and less beard.*

This Page: *Ichabod in his Colonial Army uniform.*

Opposite Bottom: *Ichabod tries contemporary clothing.*

convey something different. Maintaining that look, which started as scruff but then it became a more honed beard, it was just right for the character."

However a beard was historically inaccurate. Castellano explains, "Facial hair was actually really rare in that period. But, aesthetically, it just really works as a whole packaged look for the character. It's always something that I wrestle with, because I do have a degree in History – being historically/period accurate is fine, but we are in the business of telling a story. It's a fantasy. It's one of those instances where I understand what is 'period correct,' but what this story needed… was a beard."

Left: *A page of Ichabod's fake passport.*

Below: *Ichabod's scar.*

Look Closer

In keeping with the show's take on his character, actor Tom Mison was outfitted with a wig to create a dashing long hair style that could be tied back in a ribbon.

'*Doing our research, Crane's hat is what they wore in the New York regiment. It stuck because he looked so good in that hat.*'

Kristin M. Burke (Series Costume Designer)

Above: *Ichabod in his New York Regiment uniform.*

Above Left: *Wearing his militia clothing.*

Below: *Ichabod in formal non-military wear.*

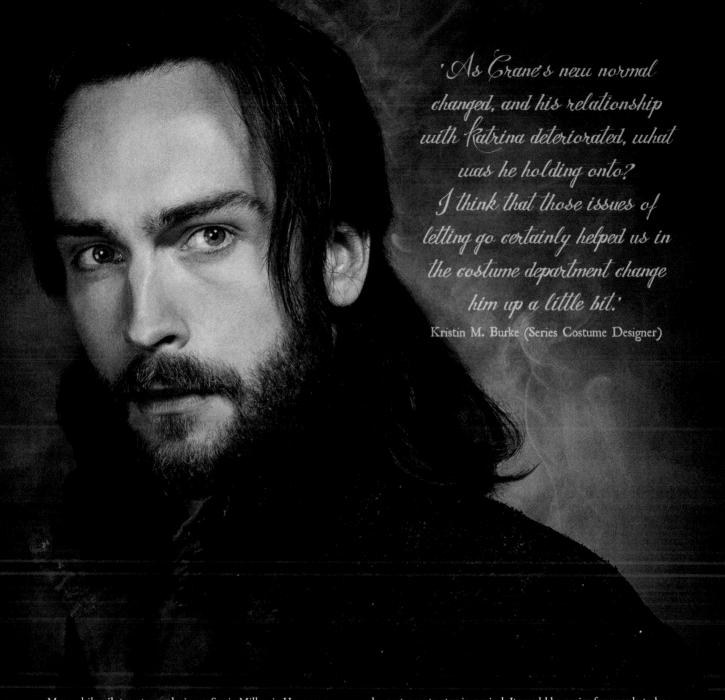

'As Crane's new normal changed, and his relationship with Katrina deteriorated, what was he holding onto? I think that those issues of letting go certainly helped us in the costume department change him up a little bit.'

Kristin M. Burke (Series Costume Designer)

Meanwhile pilot costume designer Sanja Milkovic Hays was scouring history books to find inspiration for their man-out-of-time hero. "What I thought about his costume was that it should not be so typical of that period," she explains. "I researched and found there was a New York militia of that time. With Crane being a professor, I thought he wouldn't have been a military guy. He would've joined the militia. I found this uniform, and it was a completely period uniform, but he also looked a bit like a rock star. I thought, 'I can see him looking kind of sexy in this,'" she laughs lightly. "So, the uniform, the jacket, it is of the period, but through the filter of making him look a little like a rock 'n' roll star, too."

From there, Hays says the next big decision was how to transition Crane from the cave where he is frozen for 200 years to the contemporary world. She admits thinking long and hard if he would change into contemporary clothes, or not at all. "That was the hardest thing to decide," she remembers. "My instinct, especially when we knew that Tom Mison was going to

be cast, was to stay in period. It would be easier for people to be constantly visually reminded that he is of another world."

The costume that linked both worlds turned out to be Crane's now iconic long coat which is akin to a superhero costume for which he is synonymous. "We made that coat for him," Hays explains. "Plus the shirt and everything that goes with that. I have an excellent tailor, so we were really lucky because we were able to get Tom when he was here reading for the part. We took his measurements and my tailor made his clothes for him. And he wears it so well. It's so great for a designer when a costume and an actor become one. It's not like Tom is wearing a costume – he really does become this character.

"We also made the boots for him," Hays continues, "because a lot of period boots in costume houses were kind of yucky and uncomfortable. I knew he was going to have to spend so much time in them. They were actually based on very accurate research. I try to go behind "the obvious" with something like those boots, so they're based on the period, but made especially for Tom."

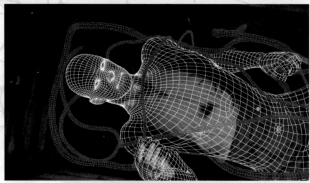

Above: *Jeremy Crane watches as his father is buried alive in the same grave that he was buried in.*

Left: *Visual effects wireframes of the climactic season one finale where Crane is wrapped in CG vines and buried alive.*

Ichabod's Cave

The cave was Ichabod's resting place for over 200 years, from his "death" in 1781, until he wakes in 2013. Katrina Crane and her coven, the Sisterhood of the Radiant Heart, laid Ichabod's body to rest in the chamber, along with a Bible in which the Book of Revelation passage referring to "two witnesses" is marked.

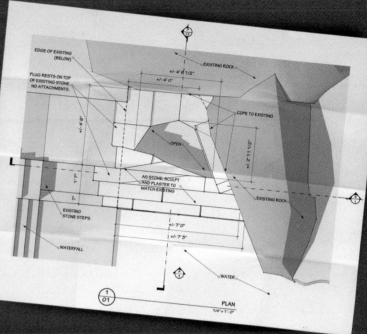

Below: *The blueprint for the cave's external location.*

Left and Below: *Exteriors of the setting for Crane's resurrection cave.*

Above and Opposite Main: *Interiors of the resurrection cave built on the soundstages.*

Below: *Two digital concept designs of the cave interior.*

Above: *Blueprint for the cave interior.*

Below: *Set dressing elements.*

The Battlefield and Triage Hospital

Having been tasked by General George Washington to find and kill the Hessian branded with the symbol of a bow on the back of his hand, Crane manages to decapitate his quarry on the battlefield, but not before he is fatally injured by the Hessian's broadaxe. Crane is taken to the hospital, where his wife is nursing the wounded, and (apparently) dies with her by his side.

Left and Bottom: *Production design photos of parts of the battlefield seen in the pilot.*

Right: *A production design photo of the dressed hospital set from the pilot.*

Below: *A digital design for the hospital.*

Grace Abigail 'Abbie' Mills

As Ichabod Crane's contemporary lifeline, eventual partner and co-Witness, Abigail Mills was crafted as a completely original character who was born and raised in the quiet burg of Tarrytown, New York. A detective mentored by her father figure Sheriff August Corbin, Mills begins the series ready to embark on a new career path with the FBI in Quantico, Virginia. But that's delayed indefinitely with the arrival of Ichabod Crane.

Mills, as portrayed by actress Nicole Beharie, is the sardonic and pragmatic foil to Crane's contemporary bluster. Athletic, assured, yet low-key, Abbie needed to be the visual yin to Ichabod's yang. An obvious beauty, the initial challenge was to modulate Beharie's look into a working cop in a small, working-class town.

Makeup department head Corey Castellano says of those early days, "When I first came on board, there was talk about downplaying her look because she's a small-town cop. But as we started getting into it, and as I started talking with Nicole, the

Left and Right: *Early concept art of Abbie Mills' police uniform.*

Above: *Two of the final uniform looks.*

'I've always loved Abbie's look. Very early on we thought it would be more interesting to see her as a plain clothes deputy sheriff, and that is something that evolved over the course of the show.'

Mark Goffman (Executive Producer)

producers, the writers and myself, we started to realize a few things. One of them was that she's a 'small-town cop,' but she was on her way to Quantico. She's not living in a vacuum. She is a modern woman," he emphasizes. "She is going to take care of herself. She is aware of fashion and different styles. So having someone who has a kind of 'done' look as a counterpoint to the rugged look that we did for Crane was a really nice juxtaposition. It visually brought out the fact that she is a modern woman; a woman of today. I really wanted that contrast."

Above: *Abbie's driver's license.*

Lori Mills

The great-great granddaughter of Grace Dixon and mother of Abbie and Jenny, Lori was tormented by demons when her daughters were growing up. Her resulting mental instability led to her admittance to Tarrytown Psychiatric Hospital, where under the influence of the demonic nurse Gina Lambert she committed suicide. After her death, her daughters discovered that she knew Abbie was a Witness and that she had knowledge of magic.

Right: *Costume design for Lori's hospital smock.*

Below: *Actress Aunjanue Ellis as Lori in the psychiatric hospital.*

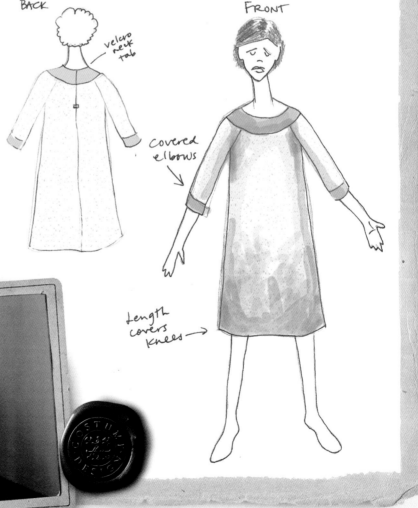

'It was freezing in January in Wilmington, N.C. where we were shooting the season two finale. Nicole really wanted to wear that jacket. We didn't want to bundle her up in this giant jacket with a hood. Then I saw some photos and thought, 'Actually, she looks awesome!' The jacket had all these zippers and it looks so unusual. It defines her in the same way that Crane had a jacket that defined him in his era. So there was a symmetry that I thought was really fun.'

Mark Goffman (Executive Producer)

In the pilot, Mills is first introduced in her uniform, which set the tone for her character's work and how she carried herself in her job. "Nicole is a very petite lady," pilot costume designer Sanja Milkovic Hays explains. "Everything that is available in the world of real sheriff's uniforms were so big that she would've looked like a clown, so we ended up making a uniform to fit her. Like for Tom, it had to be that fine line between her looking good, but not unbelievably good," Hays smiles. "We made pants that really fit her and a jacket that was her size; basically, what someone who is so petite would be wearing in that position.

"From the pilot onwards, we were then slowly making Abbie more casual," Hays continues. "It was one of the things that myself, the studio, and [the creative team] always wants: for [characters] to look sexy. However, because she's a woman in a man's world, if she's too sexy, then it becomes too gratuitous. Fortunately, Nicole is such a naturally gorgeous girl, that when we were going through different T-shirts and tops and casual wear, it was easy to add that element of sexy to her look but not make it too sexy."

Like Crane's signature coat, Abbie too was fitted for a coat that ended up softening Mills' look while maintaining the air of authority that is so inherent to the character. "When we found her leather jacket, I thought it was good for that transition," Hays explains. "I wanted her to have a jacket that looks good on her, and has a sense of style, but not too obviously rebellious. Their jackets also look very good next to one another. They just look right."

As season one progressed, series costume designer Kristin M. Burke continued to hone Abbie's look using the jacket silhouette that complimented the two characters in the frame. "I found these cropped leather coats that were more

petite in proportion," Burke details. "The initial thought was that she's a cop on a cop's budget so let's reflect that. She has basically two coats for the first season and then we gave her three or four coats that we threw in occasionally and some workout wear to mix it up. Nicole has an *amazing* figure and that's just nature. In order to feature that and not drown her we need to put her in clothes that are in good proportion to her body. She can look like she's six feet tall if we dress her right. Then when you put her next to Ichabod, who has a longer silhouette, it separates them and defines them clearly."

Below: *Abbie dressed casually to watch a baseball game.*

Westchester County Police Department

One of the show's "standing" (permanent) sets, the police station – and base of operations for Sleepy Hollow's sheriff – was constructed for the pilot episode. As production designer Alec Hammond recalls, the look of the station was very carefully considered. "Kathy Lucas, my set decorator for the pilot, was really good at finding the right amount of organic things that gave it the sense that it was at the heart of the founding of America," Hammond says. "It had a lot of the art on the walls. It felt like it hadn't had any new stuff for a long time. We made it feel like it has a deep connection to its past."

Right: *The blueprint for the standing police department set.*

Below: *The dressed set in the pilot.*

POLICE
DEPARTMENT
LOBBY HOURS
7 AM - 5 PM

*'The police station needed to feel 'small town,' so we kept an earth-
tone palette and a very monochromatic environment. We set up a series
of complicated levels and depth of dressing, giving the idea that everything
is there and available. If you walk in, you think that this is the entire
place, but the more you look at it, the more it becomes clear it is a
complicated architectural environment. Plus, the main bull-pen needed to
be a big enough room that you don't get bored of it quickly.'*

Alec Hammond (Original Production Designer)

This Page: *Set photos from the pilot featuring various locations in the police department, with digital set designs for the interrogation room (below right).*

Above: *Digital concept art of the cell where Crane was brought for interrogation in the pilot.*

The Archives

This Image and Opposite Top: *Set photos of the massive archive standing set.*

Opposite Bottom and Left: *The archives in season one's 'For the Triumph of Evil' and season two's 'Spellcaster' (top) and 'Magnum Opus' (bottom).*

'The archives are partly based on the governor's residence of Colonial Williamsburg. Those big round windows are pretty much a direct lift. For the Washington mural, I wanted a big, grand gesture to put on the other side of the archives, and a grand gesture it did make and created a rich environment. But it was also there to provide an opportunity for those clues to be woven into the fabric of the show. I love the archives.'

Alec Hammond (Original Production Designer)

Look Closer

One of *Sleepy Hollow*'s standing sets, the archives are a reminder of the American history which is an essential ingredient of the show. Though technically the property of the police department, in addition to storing police files, they also contain Corbin's files on supernatural events in the area. As a result, the Witnesses use the archives for their research and planning. As well as having an above-ground entrance, they can also be accessed via the tunnels.

Right: *Set photos of the massive archive standing set.*

The Archive

GEORGE WASHINGTON

"In the pilot, George Washington was played by the director of photography Kramer Morgenthau, ASC. It was kind of cool. When we shot him [later in season one], it was another actor, but he was 5' 9" and the real George Washington was 6' 5", so we had to figure out a way to make it work, to add at least eight or nine inches on this guy. We did it with camera tricks. There is no shoe elevator that will make someone that much taller."

Kristin M. Burke (Series Costume Designer)

Below: *Some of the books and papers, including a masonic tome (far left) and a map of Sleepy Hollow, stored in the archives.*

August Corbin

Functioning as both the sheriff and the beloved mentor of Abbie Mills, August Corbin only featured briefly in the pilot, but his presence was still felt via mentions and flashbacks throughout the first two seasons of *Sleepy Hollow*. Played with homey intensity by actor Clancy Brown, pilot costume designer Sanja Milkovic Hays says they purposefully created Corbin's look to be the most grounded and realistic of the local characters.

"We used an actual sheriff's uniform off the rack," she explains, "and we altered it for him. Clancy's such a good-looking guy that it worked so well. From the very beginning, we knew that it was a sheriff's town, not a police town, because that always feels a little more approachable."

When Corbin returned in flashback, the costume department used those appearances to fill the audience in on more of the character's backstory via his physical presence. "We had to build his backstory that we didn't see in the pilot," says series costume designer Kristin M. Burke. "He's a big guy, a burly dude and he lives in a cabin. Connect the dots. So we got some awesome hunting coats and ran with it."

Below: *Corbin's funeral.*

Left and Below: *Art department original designs for the sheriff's badge and police car.*

This Page: *Separate special effects and visual effects elements composited for the final CG sequence in "Bad Blood."*

THE CORBIN FILES

While he was Sleepy Hollow's sheriff, August Corbin investigated numerous contemporary and historical supernatural events in the area. Though they were strictly off the official record, Corbin nevertheless kept a case file on each investigation, and also collected any artifacts he unearthed and stored them in the archives or his cabin. Corbin bequeathed the files to Abbie, and they prove to be an invaluable resource for her and Ichabod.

As well as the props featured on the show, The Corbin Files is a series of approximately one-minute long YouTube videos narrated by Clancy Brown, each tying in to one of the show's episodes and released the day after that episode's original airing. They provide background to the case the Witnesses investigate in the corresponding episode.

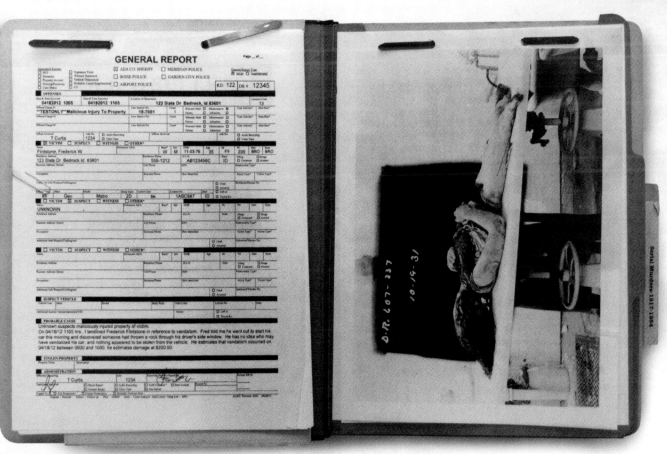

Devil-Casting Rites Cure Boy

Jesuit Priest Routs Evil Spirit

BELPHEGOR · BELZEBUTH · BERITH · BUER

CAACRINOLAAS · CAYM · CERBERE · DEUMUS

EURYNOME · FLAGA · FLAUROS · FORCAS

FURFUR · GAAP · GOMORY · HABORYM

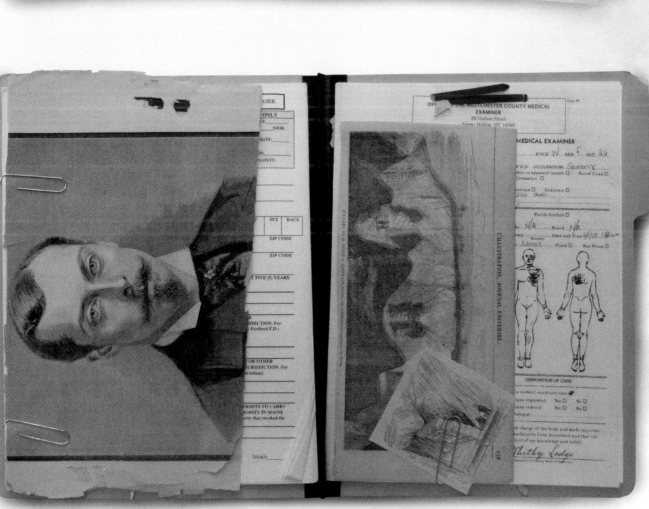

OFFICE OF THE WESTCHESTER COUNTY MEDICAL
EXAMINER
88 Hudson Street
Sleepy Hollow, NY 10599

The Cabin

"When we were considering where Ichabod Crane should live, we really put a lot of thought into it. The best place seemed like this cabin that belonged to Corbin. It could have all the secrets that Corbin held within that cabin – and even in the first episode, we found one of those – but it also felt rustic, homely, real and tangible, as opposed to a futuristic world. Ichabod chose that place as much as we did; it was set in a part of Sleepy Hollow where he could chop wood outside and feel closer to home than say, in Manhattan."

Mark Goffman (Executive Producer)

'Corbin's place has history, and that's why we put Ichabod there, to give him a connection with Corbin, even though he didn't have screen time with him. The audience also understands that Corbin was a father figure to Abbie, and the writers wanted to have a continuation of that thread that they could flash back to. The writers liked the idea that Corbin had been doing all of the groundwork, almost preparing Abbie for joining Ichabod in the crusade against evil.'

Jeremy Cassells (Season Two Production Designer)

This Page: *Set photography of the cabin exterior and surroundings.*

This Page: *The 1773 survey map of Sleepy Hollow, hidden in the sextant in the cabin, which shows the location of the stone chest containing the Lesser Key of Solomon.*

A New and Correct
PLAN of the TOWN
of
SLEEPY HOLLOW
NY

Jennifer 'Jenny' Mills

Introduced as the institutionalized younger sister of Abbie Mills, from the start, Jenny Mills was a visual metaphor for the path Abbie's life could have taken. Both girls experienced the harrowing incident of seeing a demon. They passed out and when found, Jenny was honest about the experience, while Abbie lied out of fear. The sisters were separated and their life-long rift grew. To personify that discord, pilot costume designer Sanja Milkovic

Hays sought to make a clear visual disparity.

"We wanted Jenny to start as a complete opposite to the well-adjusted Abbie, to show what can happen to two girls when they experience a trauma," Hays details. "One went one way, and the other went completely in the [opposite] direction. That was a defining thing about Jenny's character."

With the casting of the undeniably beautiful Lyndie Greenwood

Jenny Mills

This Page and Next Spread: *Jenny in action in "boy's clothes" in the first two seasons.*

Opposite: *Jenny in Tarrytown Psychiatric Hospital.*

as Jenny, the producers and production team found they had to play down that aspect of the actress to make her troubled life clear to the audience. "You put Lyndie in almost anything and she looks super pretty," costume designer Kristin Burke explains. "It would work against her character to have her look super pretty all the time so we had to really dial her back. We had to simplify and almost put her in boy's clothes to be that plausible."

"I really love the clothes that we found for Jenny as a character," executive producer Mark Goffman says of Jenny's overall look. "They made her so distinctive and fun. There's a rebel element to her look; an iconoclast. Someone who is fearless and doesn't care what people think, but also somebody who is ready for combat at any time."

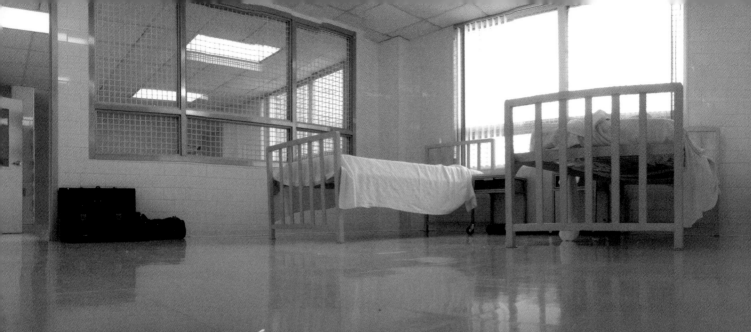

Tarrytown Psychiatric Hospital

The hospital is one of *Sleepy Hollow*'s standing sets, large parts of which were created for the pilot episode, when Ichabod was admitted and Jenny Mills was already a permanent resident. It was revealed later that Jenny and Abbie's mother had been institutionalized and committed suicide there. Frank Irving is sent to Tarrytown in season two and encounters Gina Lambert. He is also visted by Henry Parish, who tricks him into signing away his soul.

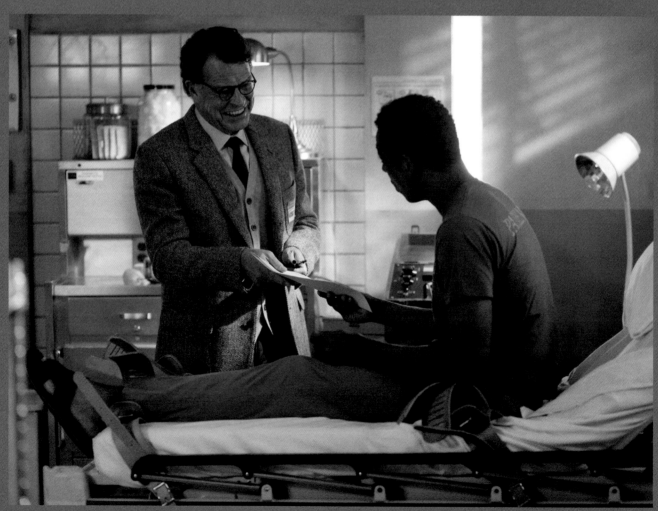

Gina Lambert

In life, Gina Lambert was a nurse who comitted "mercy killings." She was caught in 1958 and executed for her crimes. However, after death, she became a demonic nurse, haunting the same hospital where she had worked, and compelling patients to commit suicide. She was eventually defeated by the spirit of Lori Mills, Abbie, Jenny, and Nick Hawley.

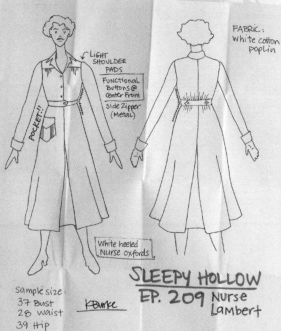

LIGHT SHOULDER PADS

FUNCTIONAL Buttons @ center Front

Side Zipper (metal)

POCKET!!

White heeled Nurse oxfords

FABRIC: white cotton poplin

Sample size:
37 Bust
28 waist
39 Hip

K Burke

SLEEPY HOLLOW
EP. 209 Nurse Lambert

'ANGEL OF MERCY' KILLER EXECUTED

Lambert Executed by Electric Chair

Patient's Death Linked to Nurse Lambert

Gina Lambert, in her Tarrytown Psychiatric Hospital uniform, her final place of employment before her arrest in '58.

Kandy, Ceylon Temple Stampede Kills 20

Hawaii Becomes 50th US State

Above: Costume design for Lambert's nurse's uniform.

Left: Prop newspaper created by the art department for 'Mama.'

Opposite Top: Production design photo of one of the ward sets created for the pilot.

Opposite Bottom: Parish tricks Irving.

Below: Production design photo of the common area set.

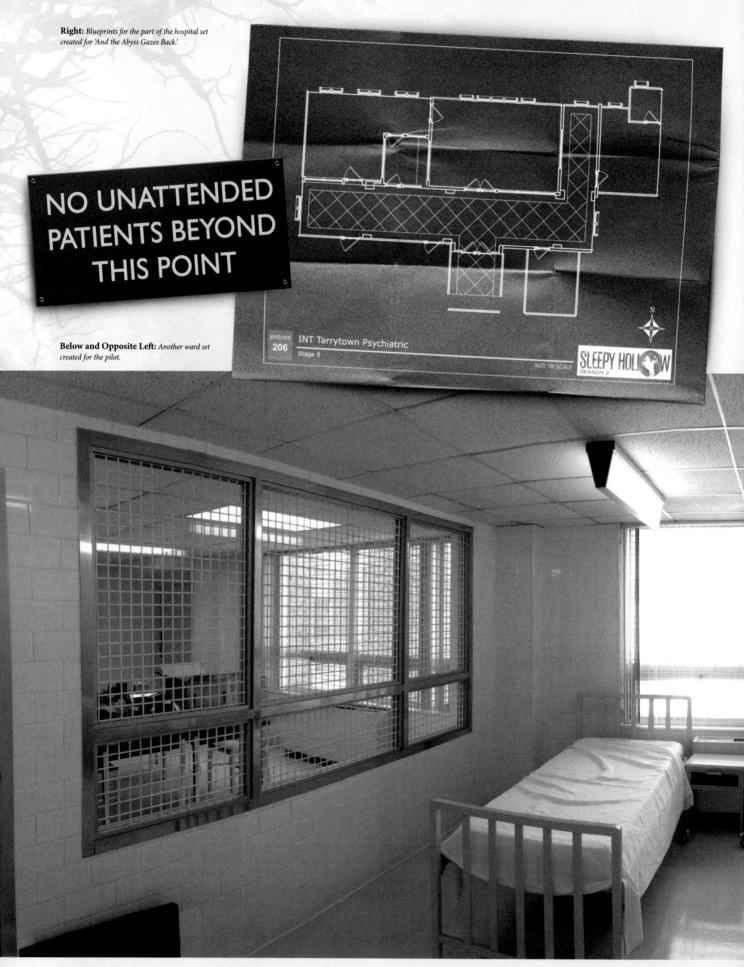

Right: *Blueprints for the part of the hospital set created for 'And the Abyss Gazes Back.'*

NO UNATTENDED PATIENTS BEYOND THIS POINT

Below and Opposite Left: *Another ward set created for the pilot.*

EPISODE 206
INT Tarrytown Psychiatric
Stage 9

NOT TO SCALE

SLEEPY HOLLOW
SEASON 2

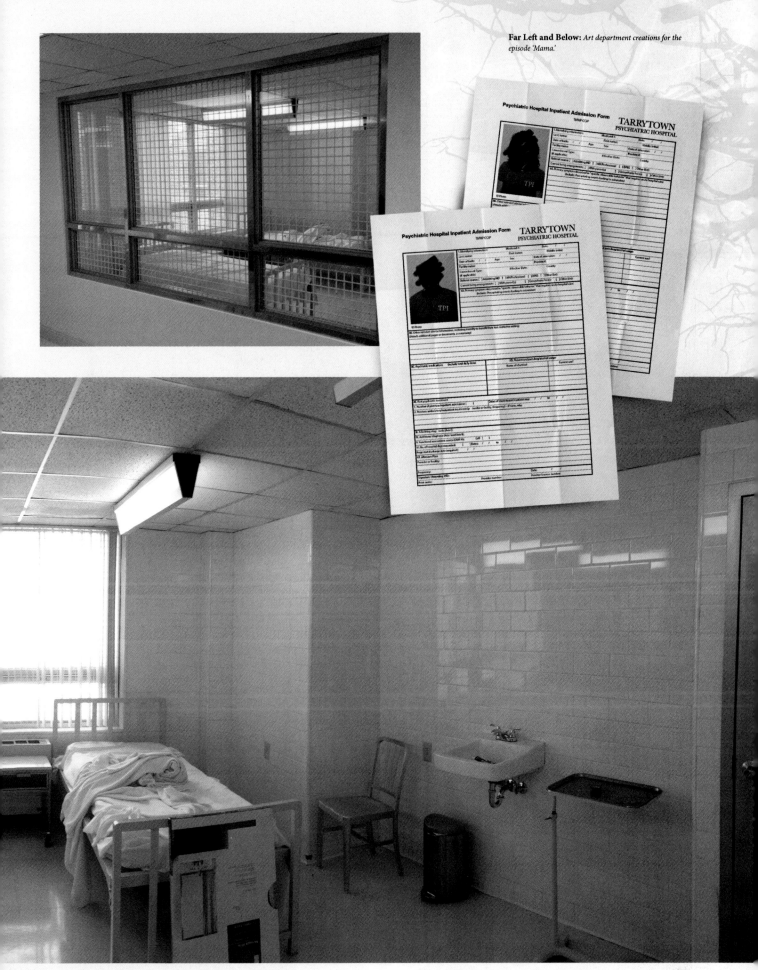

Far Left and Below: *Art department creations for the episode 'Mama'.*

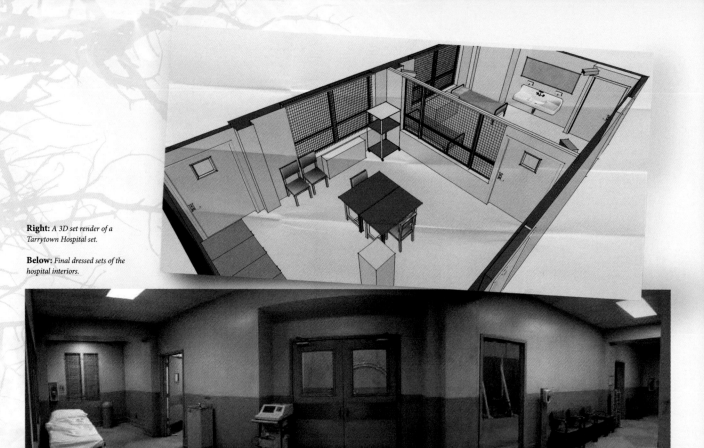

Right: *A 3D set render of a Tarrytown Hospital set.*

Below: *Final dressed sets of the hospital interiors.*

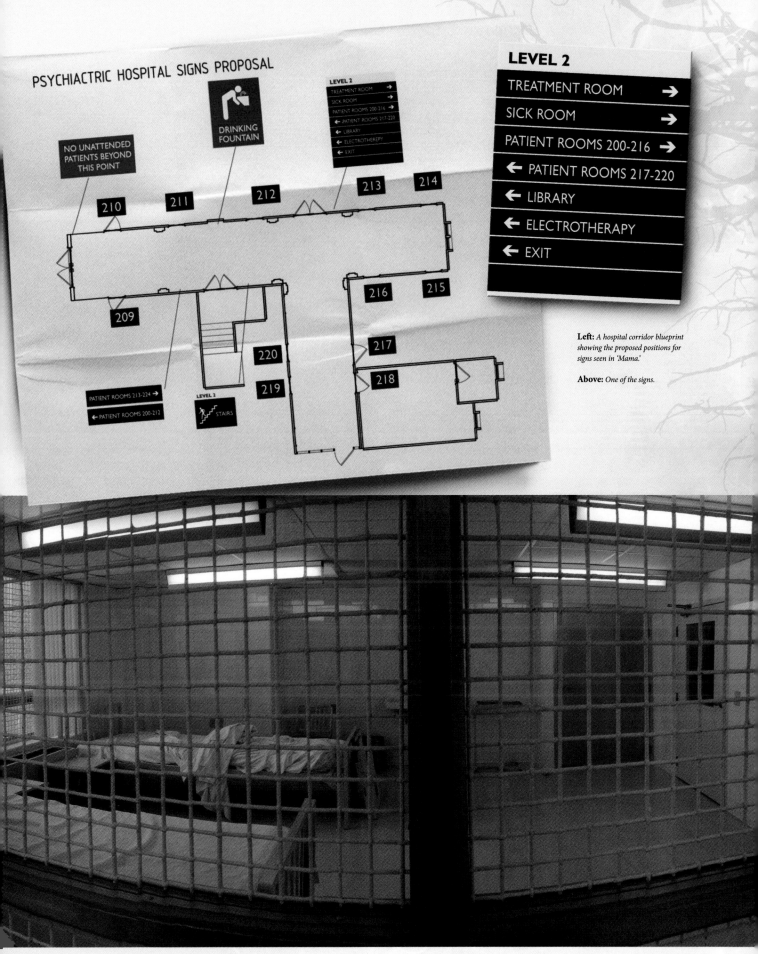

PSYCHIACTRIC HOSPITAL SIGNS PROPOSAL

NO UNATTENDED
PATIENTS BEYOND
THIS POINT

DRINKING
FOUNTAIN

LEVEL 2
TREATMENT ROOM →
SICK ROOM →
PATIENT ROOMS 200-216 →
← PATIENT ROOMS 217-220
← LIBRARY
← ELECTROTHEREPY
← EXIT

210   211   212   213   214

209   216   215

220   217

219   218

PATIENT ROOMS 213-224 →
← PATIENT ROOMS 200-212

LEVEL 2
🚶 STAIRS

LEVEL 2

TREATMENT ROOM	→
SICK ROOM	→
PATIENT ROOMS 200-216	→
← PATIENT ROOMS 217-220	
← LIBRARY	
← ELECTROTHERAPY	
← EXIT	

Left: *A hospital corridor blueprint showing the proposed positions for signs seen in 'Mama.'*

Above: *One of the signs.*

Frank Irving

With a name that's a tip of the hat to Ichabod Crane's creator, Captain Frank Irving was introduced as the voice of reason when it came to the crazy supernatural occurrences invading his town. As the chief of Sleepy Hollow's sheriff's department, he had to play skeptic to Abbie and Crane and that radiated from him from his first scene.

"He came from a bigger city, so I wanted to go with the idea that his suit is obviously perfect, like a well-dressed New York detective, not a small-town cop," pilot costume designer Sanja Milkovic Hays says of Irving's polished image. Also in keeping with actor Orlando Jones' refined taste, Hays says, "I wanted to make it perfectly tailored for him. Orlando wears it so beautifully. We then made the conscious decision to give him one look, so that would give him as an actor what he needs to let him show his character's progression. I didn't want to interfere with that."

Opposite and Above: *Irving in two of his "perfectly tailored" suits.*

Left: *The Irvings' wedding portrait, created by the props department.*

Right: *The family man with his daughter Macey, played by Amandla Stenberg, and wife Cynthia, played by Jill Marie Jones.*

61

'The biggest visual effects set extension we had in season two was when Irving has his post-apocalyptic vision. Unless you see the before and after, you can't really see what we did. It was shot incredibly, but we completely replaced the sky and added all these burnt-out buildings and the damage.'

Jason Michael Zimmerman (VFX Supervisor)

Left: *The separate visual effects layers that were blended together to create the Apocalyptic sequence in 'Go Where I Send Thee.'*

This Page: *Irving in action.*

'When Frank is on the run in season two, he is trying to hide in plain sight. You have to take a 'Bourne Identity' approach, which is to put him in clothing you don't notice at all. It's the least detailed, super innocuous and plain.'

Kristin M. Burke (Series Costume Designer)

Above and Below: *Irving dons "plain" clothes while on the run in season two.*

Left: *Irving is confronted by the Headless Horseman, who wants his skull back, in 'The Midnight Ride.'*

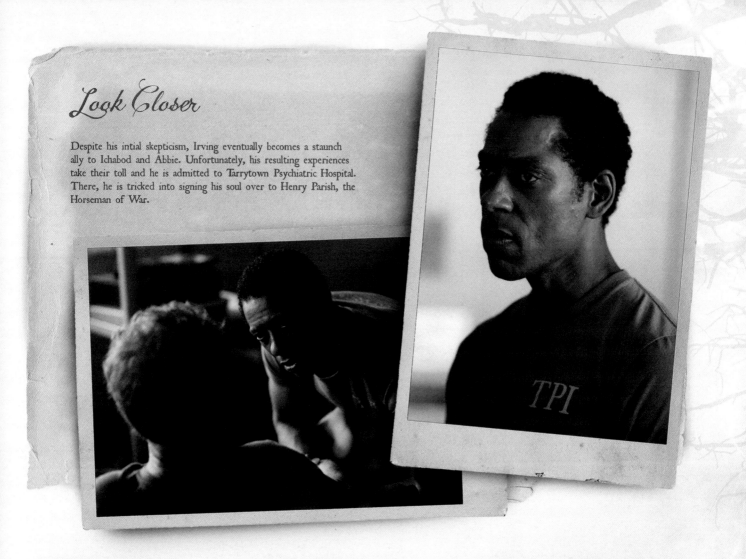

Look Closer

Despite his intial skepticism, Irving eventually becomes a staunch ally to Ichabod and Abbie. Unfortunately, his resulting experiences take their toll and he is admitted to Tarrytown Psychiatric Hospital. There, he is tricked into signing his soul over to Henry Parish, the Horseman of War.

This Page: *Frank Irving's drab look during his stay at Tarrytown Psychiatric Hospital.*

To be spoken at the entrance:
We, the penitent, with humble heart
upon this threshold do summon thee
in mirror'd form appear,
a gateway to the world between worlds.

Hudson River

surrounding wood!

surrounding wood!

Village

faithfully submitted
George Washington

The contents of this map
lead to strange and supernatural
occurances, fit only to be
set into motion by the two who will...

Purgatory

Purgatory, or the World Between Worlds, is where souls that are not immediately destined for Heaven or Hell find themselves. In *Sleepy Hollow*, Moloch appears to have control of the realm, and uses it as a prison for those souls that are key to his plans, such as Katrina. A soul can only leave Purgatory if another takes its place. The golem, Orion, and Solmon Kent all escaped, while Andy Brooks is still apparently trapped there. Katrina was freed.

The original map to Purgatory, showing the location of a doorway in the mortal realm, was hidden in George Washington's grave and recovered by Ichabod and Abbie, but subsequently burnt. However, Ichabod's photographic memory enabled him to accurately redraw the map and recall the incantation written on it that is required to open the doorway. The doorway is located in Peabody Woods.

Left: *The map showing the location of the entrance to Purgatory on Earth.*

Above: *One of the tortured souls trapped in Purgatory.*

Above Right: *A prosthetic sewn-up ear used to create the "Piano Man" Purgatory soul.*

Right: *Ichabod finds himself in Purgatory with Katrina in 'John Doe.'*

This Page: *A character concept for Katrina Crane and the final look (inset).*

Katrina Crane

A witch. A wife. A mother. Katrina Crane was a complicated woman possessing great powers that were eventually corrupted by her grief and anger. The wife of Ichabod Crane, unbeknownst to him, she was also his salvation when she used her powers to save him from the fatal wound inflicted on him by the Headless Horseman. For 200 years she was trapped in Purgatory, until Ichabod was awakened and then served as a bridge between the spirit world and the human world. As played by the lovely Katia Winter, Katrina has a stunning visage that turned the look of a traditional witch on its head.

Abraham makes another dress for Katrina that makes her look like a doll, or an uncomfortable cupcake.

Blush silk taffeta, self-trim

Katrina
EP 107

Abraham bought this dress for her - too fancy

PANTALETS

HAND FINISH, PLEASE - FRENCH SEAMS - WE WILL SEE INSIDE THIS GARMENT !!

THIN WASHED MUSLIN

Front

small shell button

Back

OPEN HERE - NO SNAPS OR OTHER CLOSURE.

30"

Light Pink silk ribbon 3/4" wide, tied in bow @ side

2 rows self ruffle

DUE 7/15

KATRINA
SLEEPY HOLLOW
EP 207

KBURKE

Busking Closure w/placket (ruched) + Lace

FRONT

LOW NECKLINE TO SHOW CLEAVAGE 1 1/2" LOWER THAN STANDARD

UNDERSKIRT SLIGHT YOKE @ waist

Less gathers @ center front waist. More gathers on sides + back BUILT IN HIPPADS

KATRINA
SLEEPY HOLLOW
EP 205

KBURKE

ruched self fabric w/Lace

Front Placket

Floral Block Print Fabric

This Page: *Costume designs and a final look for Katrina, and the necklace Abraham Van Brunt gives her.*

KATRINA

SELF-FABRIC PINKED-EDGE DOUBLE-LAYERED RUCHED RUFFLE @ ELBOW SLEEVE.

Buttons at back waist so we can pull the skirt up like a polonaise

Floral Block-Print Fabric

SLEEPY HOLLOW EP. 205

K.BURKE

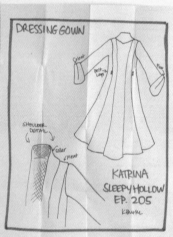

DRESSING GOWN

Collar

Belt Loop

Cuff

SHOULDER DETAIL

Collar

Pleat

KATRINA
SLEEPY HOLLOW
EP. 205

K.BURKE

This Page: *Costume designs and a final look for Katrina from season two.*

This Page: *Costume designs and a final look for Katrina from season two.*

* DULL MUTED GREEN OR TEAL FAILLE

* LINED W/ CHINA SILK IF NECESSARY

COLLAR: 4"

box PLEAT: 2'½"

PLEAT 2

CUFF

2"

3½"

6"

WAIST TIE
80"

LENGTH: TO HER ANKLES

KATRINA
SLEEPY HOLLOW
EP 205   DUE 6/23

K.BURKE

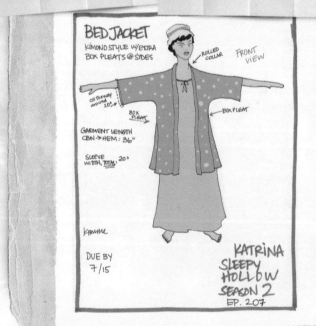

BED JACKET
KIMONO STYLE W/EXTRA BOX PLEATS @ SIDES

ROLLED COLLAR

FRONT VIEW

CUT THE WAY AROUND 20"

BOX PLEAT

BOX PLEAT

GARMENT LENGTH CBN → HEM: 36"

SLEEVE WIDTH, TOTAL: 20"

K.BURKE

DUE BY 7/15

KATRINA
SLEEPY HOLLOW
SEASON 2
EP. 207

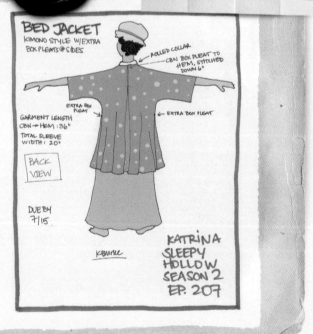

BED JACKET
KIMONO STYLE W/EXTRA BOX PLEATS @ SIDES

ROLLED COLLAR

CBN BOX PLEAT TO HEM, STITCHED DOWN 6"

EXTRA BOX PLEAT

EXTRA BOX PLEAT

GARMENT LENGTH CBN → HEM: 36"

TOTAL SLEEVE WIDTH: 20"

BACK VIEW

DUE BY 7/15

K.BURKE

KATRINA
SLEEPY HOLLOW
SEASON 2
EP. 207

Original costume designer Sanja Milkovic Hays and makeup department head Corey Castellano were tasked by the producers with creating a ravishing bride who remained out of reach for Ichabod. "For Katrina's look, we made it a little sexier than it would've been for the period," Hays explains. "We made her hair red because red heads were considered to be witches at that time. I told Len this and he thought that was really interesting."

Katrina's signature dress, which she wore for the majority of her time on the series, was a layered black dress which held visual clues about the character's origins. "Witches are always thought of as being in black," Hays explains, "but I used different shades of black and a lot of different textures. I also used alternating bronze and browns to give it a little bit of life on screen. I did a lot of distressing to the costume too, to make it look like she had been burned and had gone into Hell."

"The backstory on the Purgatory clothes is that the dress is burned," series costume designer Kristin Burke continues. "The rules of Purgatory are that you wear in Purgatory what you died in, and that was the black dress.

"Katrina was released from Purgatory but her look, even in modern times, still clung to the past. When she came to our world, she's was still wearing the Purgatory clothes. Then she is Abraham's captive and he's finding clothes for her that are reproduction 18th century clothes, because that's what he wants to see her in. Then she gets to the hospital and 'finds' clothes in the lost and found with Abbie. Conveniently they find a corset for her, which is good for the look of the show."

Castellano adds, "The visual development of Katrina over the course of two seasons was very interesting. There was a conscious effort to seed the transformation of Katrina from the time she gets out of Purgatory to the end of season two. You see her look becoming more real and more vibrant all the way through. You see the changes in her wardrobe from the flowing gowns to something more modern gothic and actiony."

'Katrina was never going to have a high neckline. Everything she was going to wear was going to show cleavage. It was the focal point of her costumes.'

Kristin M. Burke

(Series Costume Designer)

Helena Van Tassel

Hook & Eye closure in front

- Built-in Corset
- Gussets @ arms
- Trim @ cuffs + jacket edge

NO CLEAVAGE FULL COVERAGE TO CLAVICLE

Top/Jacket piece

Gusset For Free arm movement

4" CUFF

Apron
Skirt piece separate

USE A BUM ROLL for fitting. NO Built-in reQuired. we will provide petticoat + bum roll for actress

x2
DUE : 11/20
KBurke

SLEEPY HOLLOW EP 215 KATRINA (HELENA)

This Page: *The Puritan costume design and final look – showing no cleavage – for Katrina's grandmother, Helena Van Tassel, also playd by Katia Winter, in 'Spellcaster.'*

Headless Horseman of Death

"The basic idea of the character and his costume came from [creator] Len Wiseman. He knew what he wanted to do with that character and my job was really just to translate what he had in his mind to the screen. I had to make Headless larger than life. That costume was completely made from scratch. We took some creative license in creating that uniform. The color is a little higher, a little brighter, the epaulets are a little bigger, to allow for him not having a head. We wanted to put him into a world that the younger audience who play video games would recognize and enjoy, to make it a little bit stronger. We made the boots for him, and added in some lifts so he's even taller. We respected the period, and then in translation, added some elements so that he's more imposing."

Sanja Milkovic Hays (original Costume Designer)

This Spread: *Early concept art ideas for the Headless Horseman of Death.*

'It all started with Headless, and we continually referred back to Headless as he's iconic. It's a headless horseman that you've seen before, but he's wearing this awesome Hessian uniform... and then he had a machine gun strapped to his back. He was instantly iconic and massive. He set the bar for what every creature should be on the show.'

Mark Goffman (Executive Producer)

The Mark of Rheinhessen

"We had the design of the Hessian tattoo as an eight-point star, which is a star of chaos. All the producers agreed with me that just because we had this very set design, it didn't mean they all had to have the exact same tattoo in the exact same place. It's like the punks of the '80s with the anarchy symbol - there are a lot of different versions of it. So what we started doing in season two was having a variety of different tattoos, in different sizes and styles. Some looked very gothic, some looked very formal, and some looked like they had been done by a kid with a needle and an ink pen. You'll see them in different places that you might not expect, like in the crook of the hand between the thumb and the forefinger, the back of the neck, or behind the ear. It's still very cult-like, but doing different styles made it more individual to how they choose to express themselves and their allegiance."

Corey Castellano (Makeup Department Head)

'The mark of the bow comes from the Book of Revelation, but we started to create our own version of mythology, of how these elements are connected. Hessians seemed like great villains. We ran with their history, that they started as mercenaries and conscripts into the Revolution, on the British side. If the Horseman was one of them, he would certainly have followers. If he had followers then, he could have followers today, and they would be secret and walk among us. That was the inspiration for it and they just grew into the show.'

Mark Goffman (Executive Producer)

"The mask from the pilot was already made, but we had to make 15 more of them for season one. Our ager/dyer Julia made all of those masks."
Kristin M. Burke (Series Costume Designer)

'In reality, the Hessian uniform is a blue coat and red-and-white striped pants. But we thought it would be too confusing for the audience to have two guys in blue coats fighting each other. So their uniform is basically a British officer's uniform. The boots are not standard, they are Cavalier-style with a foldover.'

Kristin M. Burke (Series Costume Designer)

' You'll notice–when Headless is Headless, he's this big, huge, imposing six-foot dude. When he's Abraham, he's Neil Jackson, who is slender, with a clean uniform and it doesn't have black goop all over it. In episode one of season two, he dresses up for Katrina, her necklace beautifies what she sees. So the Headless version is dirtier than the Neil version of that costume.'

Kristin M. Burke (Series Costume Designer)

Look Closer

"When we did the pilot, we scanned Headless so we had a 3D scan of him. When we scanned the actor, he was still in the green hood. We handed that off at the time to Pixomondo Burbank and one of their artists went through and created the stump. We worked closely with Len Wiseman to make sure we had the right amount of gore and the right look. We also took high-res images of the jacket and collar and went back and forth to make sure it looked like Len wanted."
Jason Michael Zimmerman (Visual Effects Supervisor)

Above and Below: *Visual effects wireframes and final renders of Headless' exposed stump.*

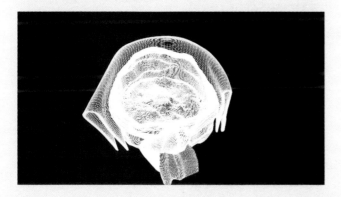 

Below: *Practical elements composited with visual effects to create the Headless Horseman's seamless final look.*

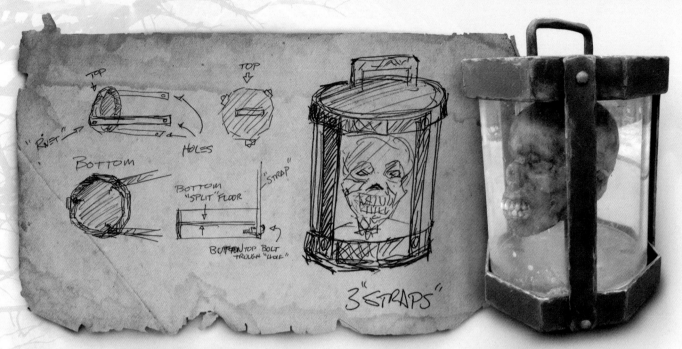

Top: *Concept art for the storage case for Headless' skull and the final prop, with skull.*

Above: *Ichabod tries to discover how to destroy the Headless Horseman's skull and the Horseman is tricked by a decoy in 'The Midnight Ride.'*

'One of the things that worked in our favor is, during Len Wiseman's early ideas, he had the concept that the Horseman of Death's axe was superheated by the fires of Hell, so it cauterizes wounds. So there is blood, but not an exceptional amount. It's a 'TV-safe decapitation!' That gave us some latitude.'

Corey Castellano (Makeup Department Head)

Right: *Headless' axe*

Gallery of Decapitations

"I coordinated with our props department and they had a number of B- or C-quality bodies we could use. We had stunt pieces that could be mounted on all of these different bodies, with three or four different qualities of heads. We could then alter them with different eyebrows and wigs to get away with different shots. On occasion we'd need something really specific, and we would do a life cast and go from there."
Corey Castellano (Makeup Department Head)

Right: *Irving, Ichabod and Abbie discover the four decapitated bodies of freemasons in 'The Midnight Ride.'*

Below: *They later discover the freemasons' heads being used as lanterns by the Headless Horseman, with candles placed in their skulls.*

Right: *The prosthetic head created for one of the Headless Horseman's first modern-day victims, Jimmy Ogleby.*

'Cutting off heads has strangely become second nature. It's become automatic. It's gotten to a point where everyone is so cool with visual effects they know what to give us.'
Jason Michael Zimmerman (VFX Supervisor)

abraham
van brunt
EP 107

velveteen coat
silk waist
coat
+ breeches

3-piece ensemble
wheat or palm frond
metallic embroidery on
waistcoat & pockets

skinny gold trim

gold trim
w/ pink
center

pewty buttons

self covered
buttons

self covered
buttons on
Breeches

COSTUME · DESIGN

SLEEPY HOLLOW
SEASON ONE

ABRAHAM VAN BRUNT
AKA HEADLESS

EP 201

Above: *Costume designs for Abraham Van Brunt from season one (left) and 'This Is War' (right).*

Right: *Early concept art for the Horseman of Death.*

'With Neil Jackson playing Abraham, what we tried to do was show a little bit of an evolution in his makeup, trying to humanise or dehumanise him, depending on what was happening. Some of it was very subtle in terms of the tone of eyebrows and eyelashes.'

Corey Castellano (Makeup Department Head)

The Carriage House

"We knew that we had to develop some kind of space where Headless and Katrina could be. We knew that couldn't be a big estate, so we came up with the idea of the carriage house. With Headless' horse, that turned out to be a pretty good idea. Then we had to go with the idea that Katrina was a prisoner there, and then that she wasn't a prisoner, she was more undercover and staying there of her own accord. We had a very cool interior. We had this very cool tree that we used for the exterior – that was an interesting little project. We also had very good plasterers who made the carriage house out of real cobbled stone and tried to give it a little bit of history, because we knew at some point we would flash back to it being in olden times too."

Jeremy Cassells (Season Two Production Designer)

Left: *Blueprints for the complete Carriage House set featured in season two.*

Above and Opposite Top and Bottom: *The design for the bottom left corner of the Carriage House set, with a digital concept and the final dressed set.*

'The carriage house was a complex set. Only Katrina, at some points, could see Abraham with her locket. There were other characters who had to communicate with him, so we had to incorporate mirrors in the set so the audience could see that it really was Headless/Abraham through the mirror. We didn't want to make the set too scary, as there was a little bit of a love story going on between the two of them. The space had to be somewhat spooky, somewhat theatrical, and have some sense of history, so you could believe that Abraham would've known about the place in olden days. Hence we went with the idea of it being an old carriage house.'

Jeremy Cassells (Season Two Production Designer)

Left: *Katrina and Abraham in the living / dining room set.*

This Page and Right: *The Headless Horseman is trapped in the hex-warded cell the Masons constructed.*

The Masonic Jail

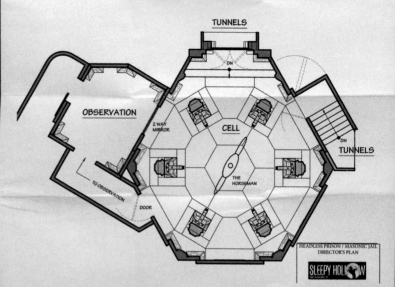

Above: *Blueprints for the Masonic jail.*

Above: *Set photography for the Masonic jail.*

'The tunnels and Headless' chamber were useful because we could also flash back to when they were older or newer and find other layers to the tunnels. They serve to add more history and a visual narrative.'

Jeremy Cassells (Season Two Production Designer)

Benjamin Franklin

Tying the past to the present often fell on the shoulders of makeup department head Corey Castellano and costume designer Kristin Burke, who worked closely with the actors cast as historical figures to create credible reproductions for the show. Castellano says that to pull that off they would focus on whatever was "visually instantly recognizable" about the figure, so audiences would connect quickly. "On television, a lot of what we do, and our counterparts in hair and costume, is helping to tell the story visually, without characters having to do five minutes of exposition," Castellano explains. "You hit elements like a hairstyle – like Ben Franklin's receded hairline and eyeglasses – which are things that are iconic and people will key in on. Not needing to have actors in prosthetics means you don't lose the actor's performance, because we haven't gotten bogged down in making them look exactly like someone else."

"People have certain images in their heads of the Founding Fathers," adds Mark Goffman. "Prior to Ben Franklin, we'd never been able to feature one that is a real character on the show. So we put a lot of thought into how to introduce him and his relationship to Crane to give a new perspective on who Franklin was and what he was like as a person."

Burke continues, "Franklin is pretty well known for a portrait where he is wearing a brown silk suit. In season one, for [actor] Timothy Busfield we made him a brown silk suit overnight, and then props gave him the glasses and makeup gave him the wig and suddenly he's Ben Franklin. As a costume department, we can provide the silhouette and the colors and shapes that people recognize."

Below: *Benjamin Franklin creates the Kindred in 'The Kindred.'*

Opposite Top: *Timothy Busfield undergoes his transformation into Benjamin Franklin in the makeup chair (left) and prepares to take an "air bath" (right).*

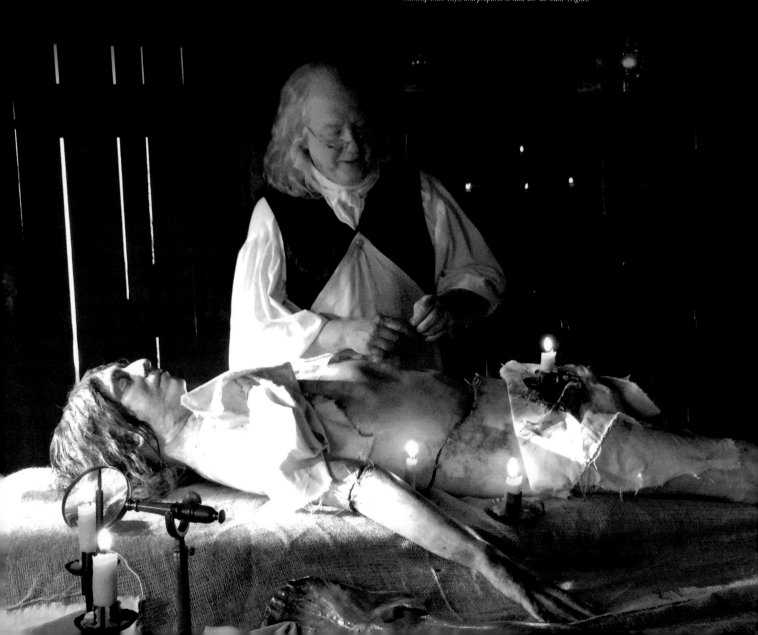

"Tom Mison is the one who told me about Ben Franklin and the 'air bath.' He was half-joking, but the more I thought about it, it seemed like, 'Well, if we're going to introduce him on this show, it's got to be memorable, fun, and we're gonna reveal more of Ben Franklin that anyone has ever seen!'"

Mark Goffman
(Executive Producer)

Benjamin Franklin

'Timothy Busfield came in for a makeup test. We did a very loose version of the bald cap on him, kicked-back hairline, added the wig, and played with a bunch of different glasses, trying to find a pair that invoked Franklin, but also suited his face. So Tim has everything on. We shifted the wig back about another quarter of an inch, and I saw a little light go off in his eyes. He settled back so he could push out a little bit of a double chin, half closed his eyes, tilted his head back, and started being Ben Franklin. It was a transformation right there in the chair.'

Corey Castellano (Makeup Deparment Head)

TWISTORY

Crane's former zany, know-it-all mentor was actually a key warrior in the war against evil. In 1775 Franklin discovered a key that can free souls from Purgatory and tried to destroy it by having lightning strike it. When that failed, he kept the Gehenna key hidden for years beneath the Sleepy Hollow clock tower, marking a cornerstone with the initials "B.F." He also built the tunnels beneath Sleepy Hollow with the help of the Freemasons. He designed the Kindred and tried to raise it with the help of the Sisterhood of the Radiant Heart coven. He knew of The Hellfire Club's plan to birth Moloch, so hid a failsafe inside the tablet in the form of a prism that can project the Aurora Borealis onto "the vessel" and prevent Moloch's birth. Franklin also hid the location of the Sword of Methuselah in a political cartoon.

Above: *Jon W. Sparks as Benjamin Franklin in 'The Vessel.'*

'The Kindred's costume was me, a fabric store, and our tailor in LA. It was quite a simple uniform, but I did custom embroidery for it.'

Kristin M. Burke (Series Costume Designer)

This Page: *Concept art for the Kindred.*

The Kindred

The Horseman of Death met his match in season two when he faced off against his own head, magically joined to a stitched-together corpse, the Kindred. "Most of the time, our discussions start with, 'We need to create a creature that's going to be the villain in the episode,' and, 'Here's the essence of what the creature is going to represent in the episode.' One that worked very much in sync with all of that was the Kindred," executive producer Mark Goffman says proudly, reflecting on its success, both visually and narratively. "The theme was Abbie and Ichabod *creating* a monster to defeat a monster."

Executive producer Len Wiseman more than planted the seed for the Kindred. "Len came up with this genius design. He actually sent me an email with an image and he'd already named it. He said, 'I call this... the Kindred,'" reveals Goffman. "We then came up with this idea that it was actually a Biblical figure in a lost Apocrypha, one of the more recently found lost books of the New Testament that Ichabod would have only been vaguely aware of. Benjamin Franklin was aware of it, but it had only been discovered

by the rest of us in the last fifty years. That became part of the storytelling. Once we had that inspiration for the creature, and Len's design, we gave it to Corey [Castellano]. The Kindred took two or three months to build and get to a point where we were all happy to sign off on it."

Although the Kindred's look is a creation of makeup department head Corey Castellano and costume designer Kristin Burke, VFX supervisor Jason Michael Zimmerman enhanced its details, especially in the battle with the Horsemen of Death and War. "We had to tackle *three* characters that all had bits of CGI. War was just a question of removing his face, Headless had the green hood, and with the Kindred, it was his milky eyes," explains Zimmerman. "The question became, 'How do we shoot this so that the green hood doesn't go in front of people? The answer is, it's impossible, because of the way the fight scene needed to be. In the end there were a few moments where an arm went behind the [green] hood, so we worked with the editors to paint it out and make it work."

Below: *Makeup sculpt and final prosthetic for the Kindred's Headless Horseman head.*

Below: *Costume design for the Kindred.*

SLEEPY HOLLOW
SEASON TWO

Echoing the lines and silhouette of Headless

Navy blue, distressed
Silver trimming & braid

Black leather gloves

Black riding boots -
Use extra pair from
Headless?

THE KINDRED
EP 202

Moloch

"The Moloch character has gone through a lot of different iterations throughout the show and that is because we – Corey [Castellano], myself and the rest of the team – really just were not happy with it. His original form was one of those situations where we didn't get the final prosthetic in costume until we were ready to shoot. I was trying to refine it even while shooting the pilot. Then we changed it and he got a little bit too muscular; a bit too big. We wanted to tone that down. We realized there was an opportunity to do that when we were going to transition and have Moloch come to Earth. The idea of him tearing and peeling and being reborn into this Earth was the moment that we were wanting to change what he looked like. I always wanted to get to a sleeker looking Moloch than the creature suit that we had and so the idea of him being in this cocoon and shedding himself like a snake became the idea that ultimately looked very greasy and worked for the whole rebirthing process for him. I am very pleased with what he turned out to be."

Len Wiseman (Executive Producer)

Left: *Season two Moloch concept art for 'This Is War.'*

Right: *Makeup application of the Moloch headpiece in the pilot.*

'When I came onto the show, after they'd shot the pilot, I was terrified of Moloch. Everyone called him 'Blurry Man' and said, 'He didn't turn out to be as scary as we hoped he would.' I was like, 'Are you kidding?!' But they had worked so hard to make him like that by adding a bunch of effects, for example, making him blurry, using quick shots and stutter editing. It was very effective. But Len Wiseman had never wholly been satisfied.'

Mark Goffman (Executive Producer)

Above: *The second version of Moloch seen in season one (left) and his revised look for the start of season two (right).*

SLEEPY HOLLOW
SEASON TWO

MOLOCH RIDES
TO WAR !!

Braided bits of leather -
Art Dept generates a symbol
for Moloch - also in lair?

cape attaches at wrist

X = MOLOCH'S
SYMBOL

COSTUME · DESIGN

Above: *The costume design for Moloch's revised look in season two.*

'We ended up scanning Moloch in the pilot, so we did a full CG version for when he is walking away from the mirror at the end of the pilot. After the pilot, we maintained the Blurry Man effect. It's a very specific blur and we developed a methodology that worked. As he changed and became different iterations, we no longer used the CG model.'

Jason Michael Zimmerman

(VFX Supervisor)

Right: *Concept art for Moloch's revised look in season two.*

Moloch Reborn

"We were brainstorming the arc for season two and at one point Len said, 'I wish I could just kill Moloch and start over.' And I said, 'Well, we actually can.' So from there, we started to work on how Moloch's goal has always been to rise on Earth. We actually came up with the idea and gave him the name Moloch early in season one. One of our writers, Chitra [Elizabeth Sampath] pitched that he be the god-demon of child sacrifice. The more I started reading about it the more it seemed to fit with how these girls had been taken in the woods and the story we were trying to tell with Abbie and Jenny. So we ran with the idea from there. We developed a much broader story than the few bars we had from John Milton's *Paradise Lost.*"

Mark Goffman (Executive Producer)

CABINET PORTRAIT

This Page: *Various views of the Baby Moloch sculpt (above right) and the final prosthetic.*

Above: *Makeup photos of Katrina's baby belly (left) and the visualization of the demonic infection.*

Below: *The full makeup design for Teen Moloch.*

Look Closer

"When we brought Moloch to Earth, Katrina's enchanted necklace gave us a really great opportunity to get around a particular production challenge. The Moloch costumes are insanely expensive, so we couldn't just build a teenage- or child-Moloch costume. The fact that Katrina was wearing this special necklace gave us the idea that, for the story, it would be really interesting to play on her maternal instincts. Moloch as a child and then as a teenager wearing Jeremy's clothes made it much more powerful and effective as to why she was unable to kill him. It also showed Moloch's rapid growth. That gave Corey Castellano the time he needed to craft a new Moloch outfit. There was one for Moloch riding the horse and another for when he was on the ground. Different actors play Moloch in those two costumes. It was an incredibly intensive process. I think the Moloch we finally saw in his full glory in 'The Akeda' was very effective and scary."

Mark Goffman (Executive Producer)

Below: *Katrina cradles Baby Moloch as he appears to her, in human form, in 'Mama'.*

'When he grows into mature Moloch in 'The Akeda' we had a lot to do with how he dies once he's stabbed by the sword. Len wanted us to come up with a different way of him dying than we usually do, like making people disappear into ash. So we played around with the idea of using electrical lights, almost like he's being lit from within by some energy source.'

Jason Michael Zimmerman (VFX Supervisor)

This Page: *Sculpts for Moloch reborn (above) and the final result (below).*

This Page: *Concept art for the reborn Moloch's adult form.*

Moloch's Lair

'Executive producer/creator Len Wiseman has a very clear vision of the show in his head, and you don't always get to it the first time, but he's very precise. We move stuff around in sets before shooting right up until the very last second. He'll always be there moving something three feet to the side, nudging a hay bale, moving something on the desk. He very much enjoys that process, which is terrific. To have a director who knows what they want and who has very clear ideas, and has so much fun with them, is great.'

Alec Hammond (Original Production Designer)

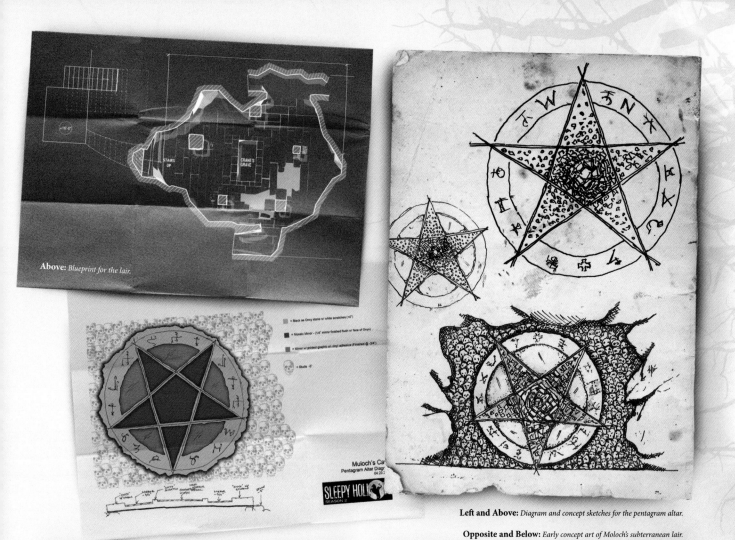

Above: *Blueprint for the lair.*

Muloch's Ca[...]
Pentagram Altar Diag[...]
04.23.[...]

SLEEPY HOL[...]
SEASON 2

Left and Above: *Diagram and concept sketches for the pentagram altar.*

Opposite and Below: *Early concept art of Moloch's subterranean lair.*

Above and Below: *The interior lair set built on the Sleepy Hollow soundstages.*

Muloch's "Altar" with Pentagram, Mirror and Skulls
04.14.2014
Muloch's Cave

SCALE: 1/4" = 1'-0"
Grid Spacing - 1 box = 1'-0"

SLEEPY HOLLOW

Center wall on (approximate) center line of adjacent cave opening

Above: *The interior lair set blueprints.*

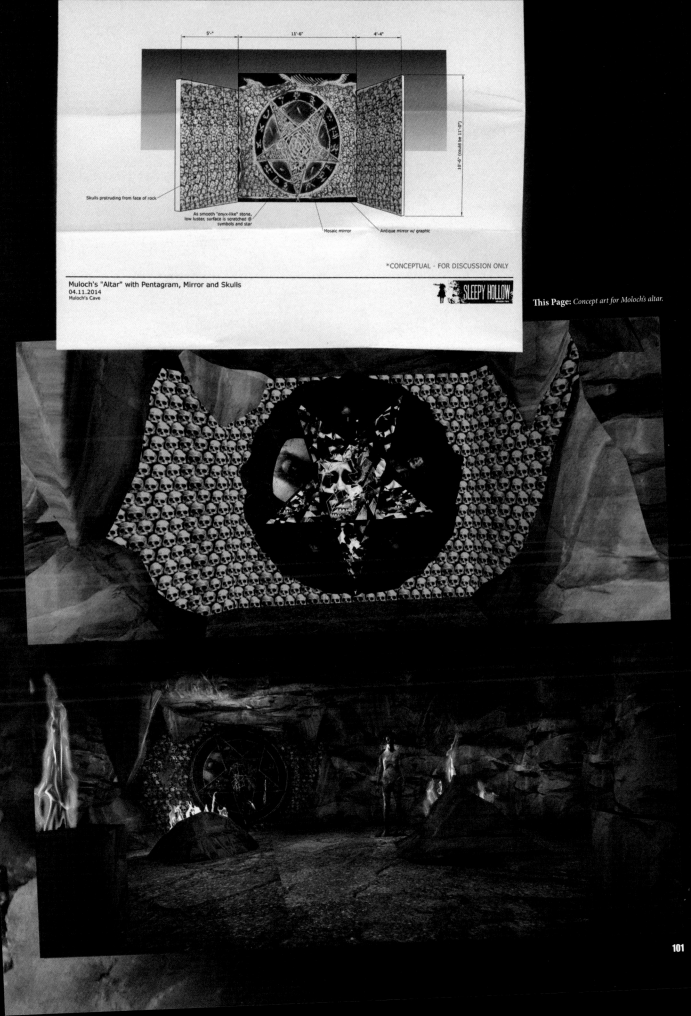

Skulls protruding from face of rock

As smooth "onyx-like" stone, low luster, surface is scratched @ symbols and star

Mosaic mirror

Antique mirror w/ graphic

5'-*

11'-6"

4'-4"

10'-6" (could be 11'-0")

*CONCEPTUAL - FOR DISCUSSION ONLY

Muloch's "Altar" with Pentagram, Mirror and Skulls
04.11.2014
Muloch's Cave

SLEEPY HOLLOW

This Page: *Concept art for Moloch's altar.*

This Page: *Jeremy Crane visits the Carriage House.*

Henry Parish and War

Introduced as the reclusive "sin eater" who begrudgingly assisted Crane and Mills with their Witness duties, Henry Parish was eventually revealed as the Cranes' lost son Jeremy and Moloch's minion, the Horseman of War.

While Parish was played by distinguished genre actor John Noble, his Horseman of War persona was realized as an imposing avatar outfit in a full suit of metal armor and chainmail. Makeup department head Corey Castellano recalls that there was much discussion on how to present War at the start of season two.

"Obviously, we had a wonderful actor in John Noble, so we had the initial idea that there was a magic pendant where you could see if he was in the armor or not," he says. "Then the idea evolved instead into [Parish] actually being consumed by the avatar of War; War was a separate thing. That way we could have the benefit of John and his performance juxtaposed with this menacing force in armor that was an equal to the Headless Horseman."

In the dramatic sequence where War is summoned, visual effects supervisor Jason Michael Zimmerman and his team

Left and Above: *Early reference armor and costume designs for the chainmail suit to be worn underneath, for the Horseman of War's avatar.*

Below: *The final visual effects-enhanced armor.*

'We only had two weeks to make the Horseman of War costume. Len Wiseman wanted something very specific. So in two weeks Legacy Effects made the costume specifically for actor Marti Matulis. They had a few armor molds and sent me pictures. Len and I, using Photoshop, tweaked their molds enough so everyone was happy.'

Kristin M. Burke (Series Costume Designer)

of visual effects vendors had to create an introduction for the latest Horseman of the Apocalypse that would rival Headless. "The toughest thing on the show is that it's a network TV show with a TV budget and timeline, but you have Len Wiseman and all of these guys with really high standards, and rightfully so," Zimmerman says of the particular VFX challenges of creating major sequences on *Sleepy Hollow*. "From season one to season two, I went in knowing the show would expand and grow and how could I help that [to happen]?"

With the first entrance of the Horseman of War in particular, Zimmerman says, "We knew it would be a big sequence for us. Mark [Goffman] landed on the idea of him bursting out of a door. So what's the best way to achieve that? Would the door be made of molten metal and he'll push his way through? It was some of my favorite [scenes] that we've done. I think we had two and a half weeks all together. It was so much fun to put it together. The sparks, the smoke and the heat distortion led to a great VFX sequence."

Left: *The full Horseman of War armor.*

Above and Below: *Visual effects CG animation for the debut of the Horseman of War's avatar in 'This Is War.'*

Above: *After being resurrected at the four white trees (set design photo, left) by Moloch – when the young Abbie and Jenny saw the demon – to take on the mantle of the Horseman of War, Jeremy Crane finds the church where he was raised (right) and takes the name for his Sin Eater alias.*

Below: *Jeremy meets his father for the first time in his guise as the benevolent Sin Eater Henry Parish (left), and poses as a lawyer to see Frank Irving in the psychiatric hospital (right).*

Above: *The miniature model of Sleepy Hollow Jeremy creates.*

This Page: *Moloch reprimands Jeremy for almost getting Katrina killed in 'The Weeping Lady.'*

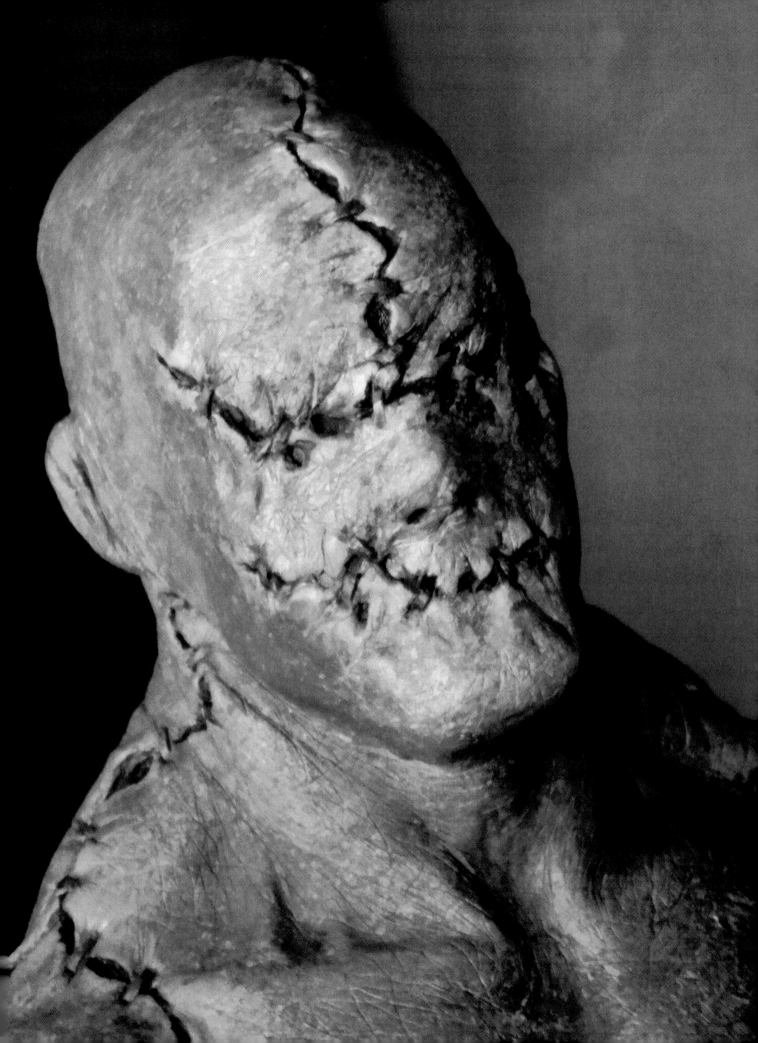

The Golem

SLEEPY HOLLOW
EPISODE 109

golem

'We were able to nail something that was disturbing and creepy, but it also had a heart to it.'

Corey Castellano (Makeup Department Head)

Above: *The costume design for the golem.*

Unbeknownst to viewers, the tale of young Jeremy Crane's doll-turned-giant protector hid one of the show's most important secrets, that Henry Parish was the Cranes' son. The episode's titular creature is one that executive producer Mark Goffman is very pleased with. "The golem was another example where the creature epitomized the theme of the story," he enthuses.

Makeup department head Corey Castellano concurs. "When I realised that it was supposed to be this doll that came to life to protect the young Jeremy, I hit upon a couple of design elements that I felt really good about. Len [Wiseman], Mark, and all of us were very involved, and there were a lot of very strong ideas about where we wanted the golem character to go. I had the golem actor Derek Mears send me stills of him in different poses and was able to do a lot of Photoshop work on him. Actually, most of my [creature] designs were done on photos of the people that were going to be playing them."

Top Right: *The golem reverts to its doll form in 'The Golem.'*

Left and Right: *Actor Derek Mears in full makeup and the final costume as the golem.*

The Scarecrow

"One [creature] that really stands out in my mind that was a brutal deadline was the scarecrow. I think we had six days to get that together. We got the final approvals on the design on a Friday, everybody cleared out of the shop, then we had to have it on set the following Thursday or Friday. That was arguably the worst one we had to deal with because it was a *big* suit."
Corey Castellano (Makeup Department Head)

Left and Above: *Actor Marti Matulis in full practical makeup as the scarecrow demon sent to Earth by Moloch in the episode 'Sanctuary.'*

Right: *The scarecrow makeup gets a retouch on set.*

Look Closer

"We cut as many corners as we could with the scarecrow, but for some parts of the process, there is just no way to accelerate them. There are often physical incapabilities between things like shipping and waiting for materials to cure. You are literally at the mercy of chemistry or physics."
Corey Castellano
(Makeup Department Head)

The Church

"It was actually a church hall that we used for the flashback. The problem was that Mark had described the church as completely rundown – that it had to be that way for Henry, and be a part of who Henry was. We couldn't go to the location church where Katrina was banished and turn it into this abandoned church. The windows in the real church were too thick to have that kind of light, where Ichabod broke the padlock, so we couldn't do that as we might have cracked the stained glass. Then we wouldn't have been very popular with the real church. So we had to quickly build it and match that and then build the internet room and have Ichabod complain about the old modem, as he's now used to our internet."

Jeremy Cassells (Season Two Production Designer)

This Page: *The final dressed set.*

Opposite Top: *The blueprint for the church interior set, and two sketches for the interior detail.*

Andy Brooks

Police officer Andy Brooks discovered that selling your soul to a demon makes for an unpredictable life *and* death. The character's undead look provided an entertaining debut task for makeup department head Corey Castellano. "Andy Brooks' busted-up neck was the first thing that was handed to me," he recalls. "We always referred to that as the 'Pez head.' Rolled up underneath that was Brooks' 'accordion neck.' We wanted to straddle a line between being disturbing and a little funny, but in a creepy way."

Brooks' snapped neck was achieved by a combination of the special makeup effects team, and VFX supervisor Jason Michael Zimmerman's group. Castellano explains, "We had the whole 'head hanging off the back of the neck' as a prosthetic, and then had a green hood on the stunt man." Zimmerman continues, "When Brooks wakes up with his head backwards, the stuntman's hood could be painted out. It was a case of removing a green head and putting a new one on there. We tracked it with 2D projection back onto the face so we see John Cho's face reacting."

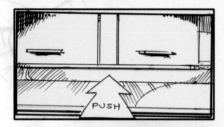
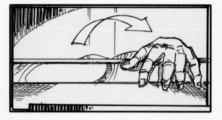

This Page: *Storyboard progression of Brooks' reanimation and the final result (below).*

Opposite Top: *The sequence of visual effects elements and stages used to create Andy's broken neck, with actor John Cho.*

'Coming up with that neck rig was pretty elaborate.
We had to make sure the way it was cantilevered all the way back
wasn't choking our stuntman to death.'

Corey Castellano (Makeup Department Head)

Left and Below: *The sculpt and final special makeup effect used to create Andy's broken neck.*

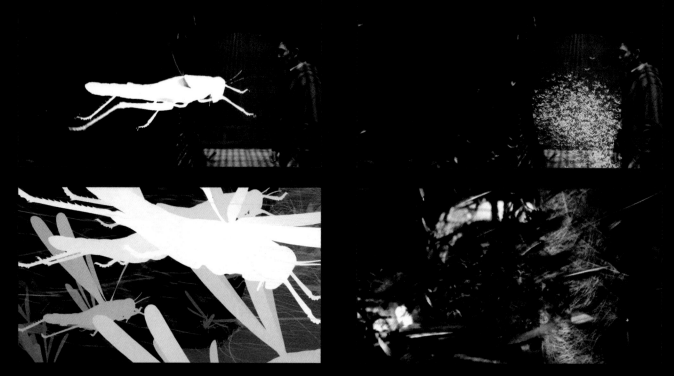

This Page: *Some of the visual effects stages for the creation of the locust swarm and Andy's transformation cocoon (above) and the final result (below).*

'The locusts were part of Brooks being reborn. We shot the sequence with John Cho where the locusts would come in and swarm him, with a series of cocoon pieces. As the locusts were swirling his legs, there were three stages that he could be covered up, so for each stage he would walk back and we would add new locusts. We animated that and covered it up with additional webs. We worked with everyone to get a realistic feel.'

Jason Michael Zimmerman (VFX Supervisor)

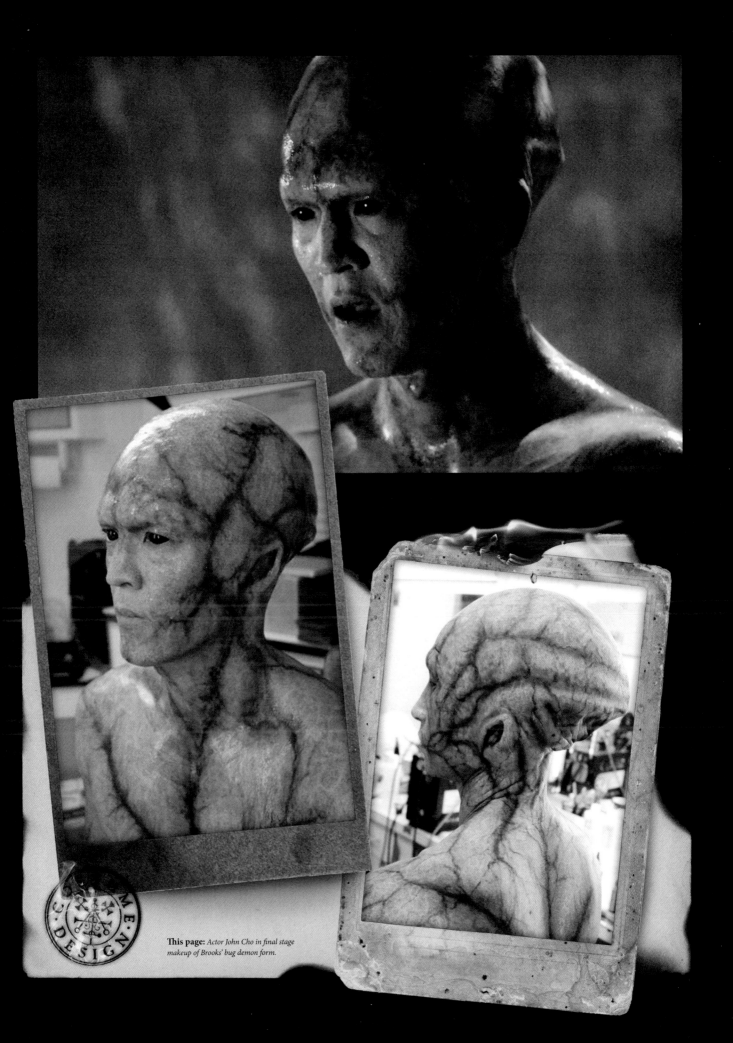

This page: *Actor John Cho in final stage makeup of Brooks' bug demon form.*

Acolytes of Moloch

Moloch's demonic followers are each branded with a different demonic mark on their chest. Apart from body paint, their look was achieved with facial prosthetics for the forehead, nose and ears, false teeth, colored contact lenses and prosthetic finger extensions.

'I had the resources to do what I needed to do, or what I felt was right, for the development of all the show's creepy characters.'

Corey Castellano (Makeup Department Head)

This Spread: *The final results of the prosthetic work.*

119

Serilda of Abaddon

*S*leepy Hollow's (first) season of the witch didn't just feature the Purgatory-trapped Katrina. Following Headless' terrifying introduction in the pilot, Moloch's resurrected old crone was anything but ordinary. "When conceiving Serilda, we put a lot of thought into what our witch would look like," emphasizes executive producer Mark Goffman. "She needed to be someone who is sexy, tortured, iconic, and a witch you've never seen before. Our witch had a very specific story that could only be told on *Sleepy Hollow*."

'The initial design artwork had already been done for the burnt witch Serilda, but I supervised that through Todd Masters' SFX shop.'

Corey Castellano (Makeup Department Head)

Above: *Actress Roxy Olin in the Burned Serilda makeup.*

Below: *Actress Monique Ganderton as Serilda.*

Above: *The costume design for Serilda before she is burned.*

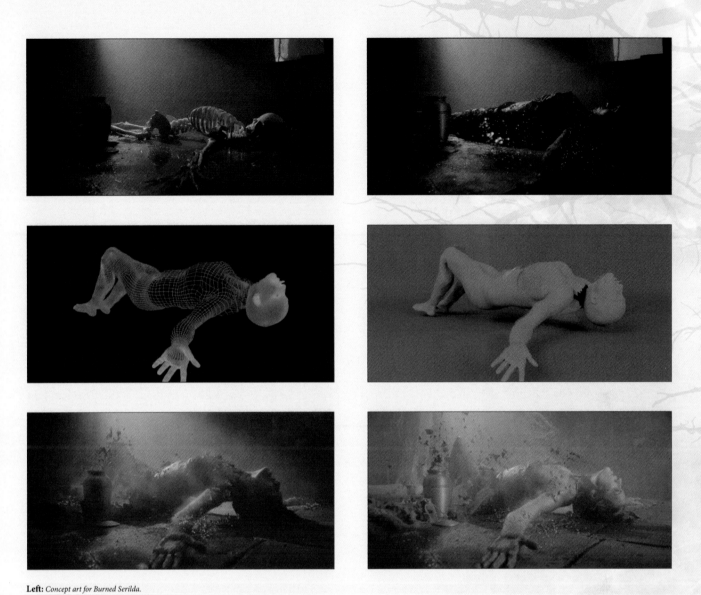

Left: *Concept art for Burned Serilda.*

This Page: *Visual effects image progression of Serilda from skeleton to fully resurrected form.*

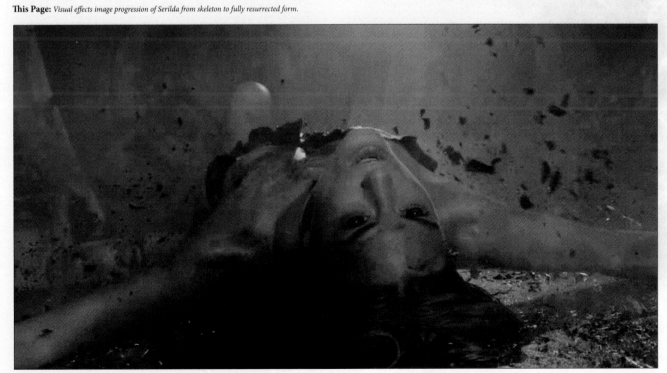

The Tunnels

'It was about establishing areas that we could revisit. The tunnels also allowed us to get anywhere without walking around the streets, and be wonderfully theatrical with 200 years of roots coming down into this subterranean place that could be anywhere. Creating a sense of 'possibility' in the environments was a great opportunity. I was very happy with the cave and the catacombs in the permanent sets.'

Alec Hammond (Original Production Designer)

The tunnels have been key to the world of *Sleepy Hollow* from the beginning. On a practical level they enable Ichabod and Abbie - and other characters and creatures - to move quickly from one location in the town to another without being seen. A literal underworld and a reminder of the dark forces that are surfacing in the town, they also embody one of the main themes of the show, that as with many small towns, there's more to Sleepy Hollow than is apparent on the surface.

Below: *Blueprint for the tunnels set.*

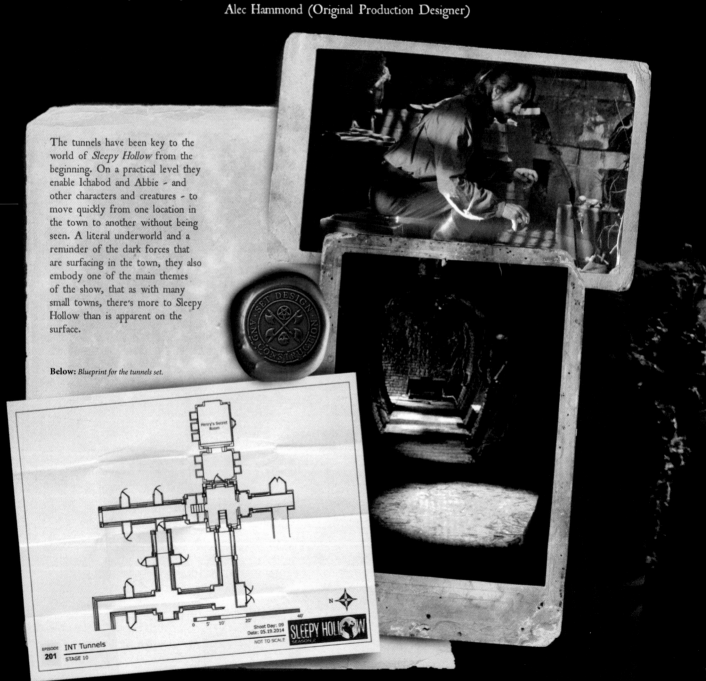

This Page and Opposite Right: *Sections of the final dressed set.*

'The tunnels are an interconnective tissue that keeps all of the different places alive. It allows our characters to move around and arrive at various places in Sleepy Hollow.'

Jeremy Cassells (Season Two Production Designer)

This Spread: *Sections of the final dressed set.*

Ro'kenhronteys

"With the Sandman, we were very lucky," explains executive producer Mark Goffman. "We were all looking around, and [makeup department head] Corey Castellano had worked with the actor Marti Matulis previously. Jose Molina, the writer of that episode, knew of him too and instantly knew he was the right kind of actor to pull off this very scary and authentic kind of demon."

The design and behavior of Ro'kenhronteys left a deep mark with many *Sleepy Hollow* fans, something Castellano has a good explanation for. "These types of demons seemed to resonate with a lot of viewers because there's so much identifiable human biology there that has been removed," he posits. "The Sandman is human-looking, but his eyes have been done away with. He's got no mouth. It's so creepy because there is so much there that you recognize, next to so much that you don't."

This demon's (literally) shattering demise was only possible with CGI (computer-generated imagery), something that visual effects (VFX) supervisor Jason Michael Zimmerman

understood the challenges of. "You are handing off from a practical person in a room to completely CG glass, which could go badly. The light had to match, but all of the departments helped so much. We were able to go in and shoot detailed images of the environment so we could reproduce the reflections, and properly reproduce the light created by the director of photography."

Left: *Final sandman makeup.*

Below and Bottom Right: *Concept designs for the sandman.*

Bottom: *Frequent* Sleepy Hollow *demon actor Marti Matulis has his sandman makeup retouched on set.*

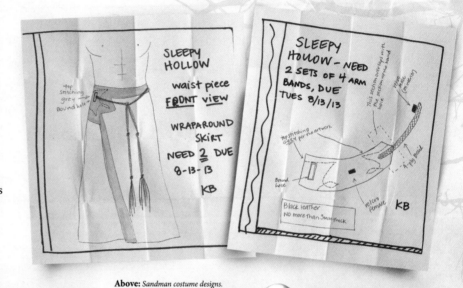

Above: *Sandman costume designs.*

Banastre Tarleton

'We would have a creature call, and we would spitball where everything needed to go for the next three episodes. We're on an eight-day schedule for an episode, so that's 24 days for three creatures. It's kind of unheard of. In film, that's ridiculous. In television, it's just painful.'

Corey Castellano (Makeup Department Head)

Above: *Concept art for Tarleton's demon form.*

Left, Right and Below: *Actor Craig Parker in Tarleton's final demon makeup and costume.*

TWISTORY

Crane was an officer of a faction of Redcoats policing Dorchester Heights, Massachussets, in 1771, under Tarleton's command. Tarleton headed an arrest party that detained Arthur Bernard, a freed slave accused of writing treasonous pamphlets under the pseudonym "Cicero" in order to instigate Colonial rebellion. Driven by his conscience, Crane eventually released Bernard against orders, and Tarleton shot Crane. When Crane retaliated by running Tarleton through the stomach with his sword, the colonel shapeshifted into a demon and hit Crane with superhuman strength, gravely injuring him before running off into the night. Tarleton was the first demon Crane encountered and the experience helped Crane make his decision to join the Colonists against the British.

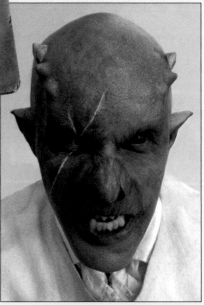

Ancitif

Moloch's accomplices came in many forms. One of the most insidious was Ancitif, the demon that can literally take on *any* form by possessing (and body-jumping between) human hosts.

Makeup department head Corey Castellano's experience of demonic possession and exorcism came with its own race against time. "We had another truncated timetable because we would lose the actress/stunt woman for part of the schedule. I think [the prosthetic] Ancitif demon was a four-day turnaround. With all of those situations, it's just a matter of getting in, doing what you can, and hoping for the best. We would have the first AD [assistant director] push the shoot of those sequences to as late in the day as possible because we'd be waiting for these still dripping-wet pieces to be ready to put on somebody's face."

Left and Above: *Corbin exorcises Ancitif from Jenny.*

Look Closer

"We had a good idea of where we wanted to go with the first stage of possession because we didn't want to use anything prosthetic. We wanted to use highlight, shadow, and color to apply the creep factor. It was a matter of balance and not taking it too far and losing the humanity from either Macey, Irving, or Jenny. We had to subvert a level of recognisability and make them look a little bit ill."

Corey Castellano
(Makeup Department Head)

Right: *Possessed Macey actress Nydia McFadden models the late-stage prosthetics.*

The Pied Piper

❝ We've all seen what the Pied Piper [of Hamelin] looks like, and you can do a web search for it. But what is it going to be like if *we* do a version on *Sleepy Hollow*?" executive producer Mark Goffman says, recalling the essence of the discussion on the show. In fact, that question fuels a lot of their creative decisions. "It had to have a very specific feel that put it in our world. It had to relate to Ichabod Crane and the Revolution. I really thought our Pied Piper worked very effectively. It was also a great collaboration, with [makeup department head] Corey Castellano, the wardrobe department, and all of the team designing him."

Heading up the wardrobe team, costume designer Kristin Burke was inspired by a 2001 French film which Len Wiseman admires. "Len very much is a fan of [Christoph Gans'] *Brotherhood of the Wolf*. In that film you see this style of jacket, a highwayman coat, in action. Looking at that film and that style, Len was asking if we could make him a 'military guy gone bad.' So we created his uniform [in that style] and aged it down."

This Page, Clockwise from Above: *Costume concepts for Sleepy Hollow's Pied Piper; The final look; Head sculpt for the Pied Piper's facial prosthetics; The Piper's highwayman coat costume design.*

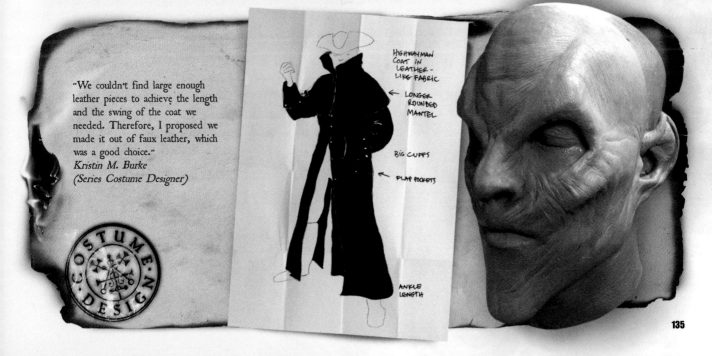

"We couldn't find large enough leather pieces to achieve the length and the swing of the coat we needed. Therefore, I proposed we made it out of faux leather, which was a good choice."
Kristin M. Burke
(Series Costume Designer)

HIGHWAYMAN COAT IN LEATHER-LIKE FABRIC

← LONGER ROUNDED MANTEL

BIG CUFFS

← FLAP POCKETS

ANKLE LENGTH

This Page: *Comparison of concept art and final look with actress Heather Lind.*

The Weeping Lady

The tragic spectre of Mary Wells gave the makeup, wardrobe, and VFX departments a very different "monster" to create. "Even though she wasn't a 'demon' per se, I'm pleased we were able to maintain a feel and a design ethic with this ghost," recalls makeup department head Corey Castellano. "I think we've managed to do that with all of the different otherworldly characters, which is not always easy."

This consistency of tone, and the specifics of Mary's fate, meant costume designer Kristin Burke and her team had a lot to consider. "We had early meetings about drowned people and what they looked like. This was the most important thing to establish," emphasizes Burke. "Next, they wanted something that looked black. However, in the 18th century, black was not something people wore unless they were mourning. There would be no reason for her to be mourning, as she was pursuing Ichabod as a husband!" she points out. "So I had to take some liberties to get black into her costume. Because she's kind of an obnoxious character, I made her into a sartorial dilettante."

Design aside, actually making Mary Wells' costumes ended up being a sprint to the finish line. "We didn't know Heather Lind would play her until four days before shooting… but these kinds of costumes take three to four weeks to make," recalls Burke. "We can rent some clothes, but as they needed at least three of the original Mary Wells gold-colored dresses, and three or four of the Weeping Lady dresses, the petticoats, the gloves and the hat… We had to make it all."

To give this apparition an extra terrifying quality, VFX supervisor Jason Michael Zimmerman provided the haunting, watery effects. "The core, practical design was great to begin with and the better something starts, the better it ends up. In the case of Mary Wells, after talking with them and discussing what we could do to make her scarier, I pitched the ink-in-water look. Zoic did the effects and it looked perfect. Everybody was excited about it and it added a really creepy edge to her."

Below: *Costume designs for the Weeping Lady (left) and Mary Wells (right).*

'The lace cape that she wears had to be a very particular lace that is recognizable to Ichabod when he sees it from Abbie. We looked all over for it, and found the best price and look came from England.'

Kristin M. Burke (Series Costume Designer)

The Wendigo

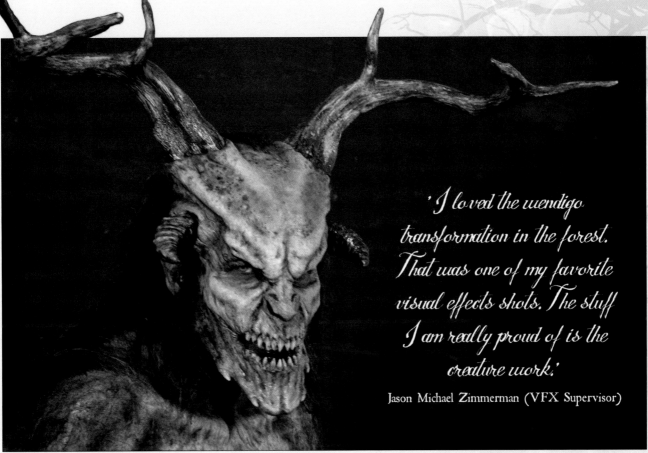

'I loved the wendigo transformation in the forest. That was one of my favorite visual effects shots. The stuff I am really proud of is the creature work.'

Jason Michael Zimmerman (VFX Supervisor)

Left and Above: *Final head prosthetics for the wendigo.*

Below: *Actor Robin Strasds as Daniel Boone.*

Below: *Costume design for Daniel Boone's hat.*

SLEEPY HOLLOW EP 206 DANIEL BOONE HAT

SIDE VIEW

rough-out skin

TOP VIEW

6-POINT ROUGH-OUT CROWN

KBURKE

DANIEL BOONE

A militia officer during the Revolutionary War, which is how Ichabod came to meet him, the famous American pioneer and frontiersman lived with a Shawnee hunting party in 1778 in the hopes of learning a cure for the curse of the wendigo. Boone believed his brother was cursed after Squire Boone tried to eat him during Valley Forge. He wore his coonskin cap to cover the scars his brother left.

'With the wendigo, they were able to achieve a completely practical creature that looked incredible, but we had to see him transform from Joe Corbin into the wendigo. We scanned what Corey Castellano had done and did a full computer-generated transformation. Some things like having the wendigo jump off of a building and parkour off a light-post couldn't be done practically, so we did those CG too.'

Jason Michael Zimmerman (VFX Supervisor)

Above Left and Right: *A sketch and a digital art concept design for the wendigo's final look.*

Right and Above Right: *Sculptures for the wendigo's head prosthetics.*

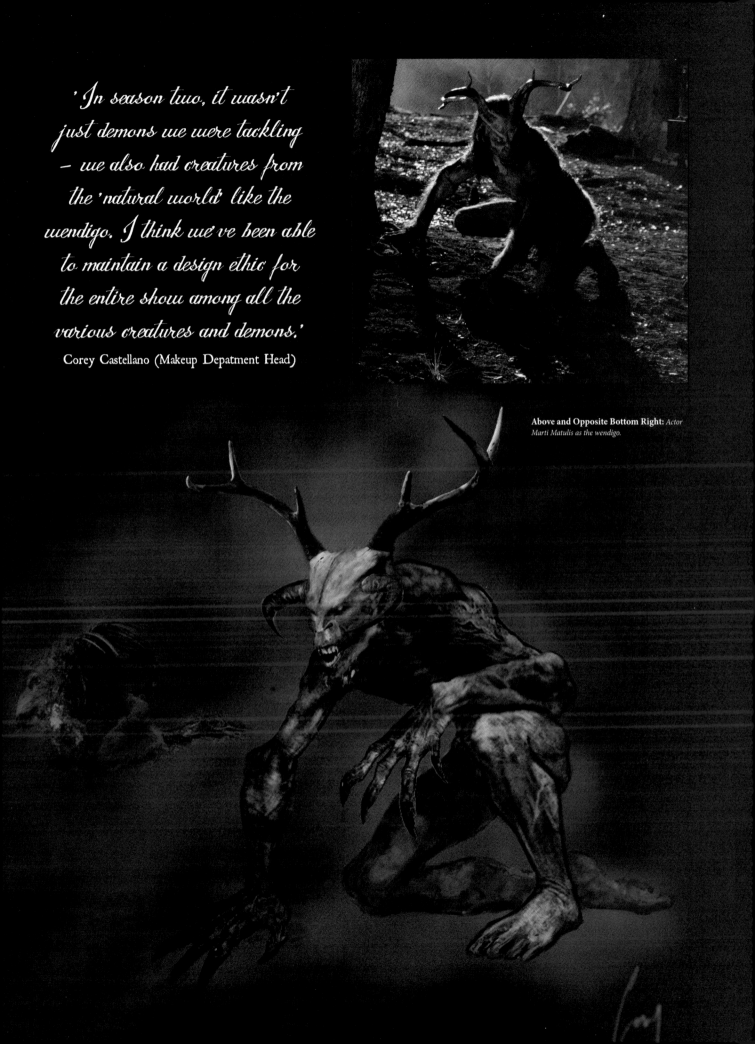

'In season two, it wasn't just demons we were tackling — we also had creatures from the 'natural world' like the wendigo. I think we've been able to maintain a design ethic for the entire show among all the various creatures and demons.'

Corey Castellano (Makeup Depatment Head)

Above and Opposite Bottom Right: *Actor Marti Matulis as the wendigo.*

This Page: *Actress Elena Sanchez as the demonic succubus.*

Right: *Sculpts for the demonic succubus head prosthetics.*

The Succubus

In 'Heartless,' a succubus is summoned by Henry Parish to gather life forces for Moloch's plan to enter the human plane. The episode's title is a translation of "Incordata," one of the demon's names, along with Lilith. Her demonic form was created through the collaborative efforts of makeup and costume.

"The succubus was played by Caroline Ford, who is a very attractive woman, who turns into something very unattractive," makeup department head Corey Castellano explains. "We had to make sure the actress was comfortable with certain elements that will get us to a final look, such as lenses, nails, and teeth."

Below Left and Right: *Concepts for the demonic succubus.*

As for the Incordata's clothes, costume designer Kristin Burke recalls the creature being particularly challenging because of her multiple looks. "Here is a monster who impersonates the object of desire of her victim, so she has to change clothes. She had more than eight costumes, and she also needed a neutral costume for when she wasn't impersonating anybody, and then she had a costume for when she is the demon. Len Wiseman wanted her in something like a black slip when she was the succubus. We also needed to translate that into when she's not a succubus. So we made the slip and needed all kinds of copies."

Below Middle: *Costume design for the demonic succubus' black slip.*

The Gorgon

In 'Magnum Opus,' Ichabod and Abbie came face to face with myth made flesh. Creating *Sleepy Hollow's* Gorgon was a combination of efforts by makeup department head Corey Castellano's team, plus some VFX reptilian enhancements. "First, we scanned the Gorgon [makeup effect] and created a CG version so we could match it," explains VFX supervisor Jason Michael Zimmerman. "Corey and Len [Wiseman] had very specific ideas about this character. They thought about doing the snakes practically, but they wanted to have a lot of hero moments where the snakes were performing too. With the snakes being CG, some of the shots were close to the camera, so we had to do higher resolution shots. There were even some wider shots that were full CG when the Gorgon picks Headless up."

Below and Left: *Early sculpts for the intricate Gorgon prosthetics, and the final head prosthetics.*

Left: *Props pages from the book that contains details about the Sword of Methuselah.*

Below: *Concept sketch for the Gorgon's flowing snake hair style.*

The Gorgon's Lair

"We really needed to use existing sets [for the Gorgon's cave], so that was actually Moloch's cave changed over. We moved some elements out, built the staircase, and then created a canvas – in our vocabulary of architecture – that had other heroes that had used sword fighting to try and get the Sword of Methuselah. We also repurposed the vault that we'd used before. A lot of this is because we just don't have the time to build these very complicated sets from scratch as a lot of it is detailed stone work. But it was a really fun set to make, because it featured our characters on a little bit of a *Raiders of the Lost Ark*-style quest."
Jeremy Cassells (Season Two Production Designer)

This Page: *The final set, with a view of the sword chamber.*

Above: *Concepts for elements of the Gorgon's lair.*

Below: *Blueprints for the Gorgon's lair, and the set under construction.*

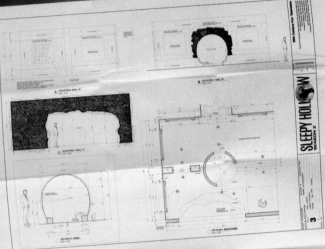

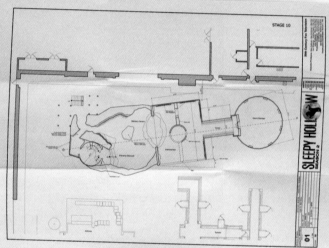

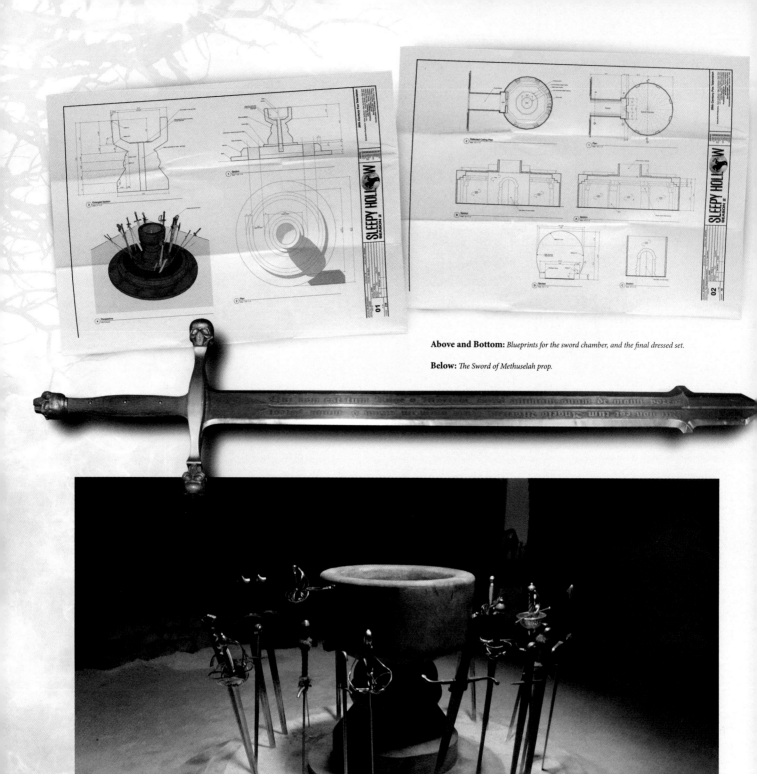

Above and Bottom: *Blueprints for the sword chamber, and the final dressed set.*

Below: *The Sword of Methuselah prop.*

Above: *A digital concept painting for the sword chamber.*

Right and Below: *Unpainted prop statues of victims of the Gorgon, and a finished statue in situ on the set.*

Zombie Redcoats

For a show that embraces the undead so frequently, is was only a matter of time before a zombie outbreak plagued the town of Sleepy Hollow. 'The Akeda' saw zombie Redcoats fight for Moloch's reign, something costume designer Kristin Burke was already well prepared for. "Fifty zombie Redcoats were originally going to be heavily featured in the second season opener," she reveals. "We had all of these costumes made so we could destroy them, because we can't destroy rentals. It's ten times the rental charge if you damage a costume. It was all hands on deck. They looked awesome, but that was only possible with us all working together."

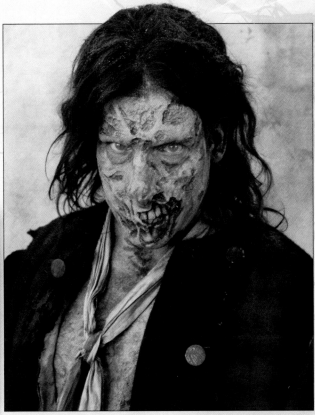

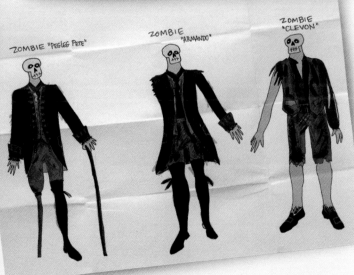

Above: *Zombie prosthetics before final makeup application.*

Above: *Zombie Redcoat costume designs.*

Left and Right: *Final zombie Redcoats with full makeup.*

Orion

In season two, it's fitting that the Horseman of Death is hunted by the Angel of Death. As an 'angelic' entity, how to approach Orion's wings became a focus for both effects departments. "We knew if Orion was flying, that was going to be us," explains visual effects supervisor Jason Michael Zimmerman. "But I like the idea of not immediately reverting to a CG character, and trying to achieve as much as we can practically. It's about working in tandem with [makeup deapartment head] Corey [Castellano], who shows me his concept art. He will do a lot of the early talking with Len [Wiseman]. Corey takes his first stab at it, and once he has, we start to talk about what VFX we need to do, if anything, for the creature."

During those discussions, one idea was to ignore flight altogether. "At one point there was talk about having him be a wingless angel, because Moloch had torn his wings off in battle," reveals Castellano. "It sounds cool, but we'd kind of seen visions of that before, so we just gave him a couple of scars and made him a bit more rugged. Orion has a very military hairstyle, a very Centurion look. It was just a matter of making him look tough. With Max Brown's performance, he was also able to bring a level of accessibility to the character."

Left and Below: *Costume designs.*

Bottom Left: *Actor Max Brown in the final Orion costume (sans makeup and wings).*

Bottom Right: *Orion's chakram props.*

The Daevoli

Like Moloch's acolytes in 'Necromancer,' the daevoli are a version of the basic *Sleepy Hollow* demon, so their look reflects that. The forehead ridges, horns, fangs, and claws are then varied slightly for each to give them an individual character.

Below: *Daevoli tabard costume designs.*

Above and Below: *The final look for the daevoli, with prosthetics, makeup and costumes.*

SLEEPY HOLLOW EP 212
DAEVOLI SLEEVELESS TABARD
DUE 10/15
× 2   size XL

FINISHED MEASUREMENTS

RED LINING ALL OVER

HOOD

FRONT

KRISTIN BURKE

SLEEPY HOLLOW EP 212 DAEVOLI SLEEVELESS TABARDS
HOOD →
DUE 10/15
×6 TOTAL
2 size XL
4 size L

SIDE VIEW: HOOD + SLIT @ SIDE

BACK VIEW: HOOD + CENTER BACK SLIT

Kristin Burke

James Colby's Artist's Loft

The supernatural ability of Colby leaving and re-entering his macabre painting gave VFX supervisor Jason Michael Zimmerman more than a few technical challenges. "I was scratching my head about how we would do it. We sat down and came up with a solution where the painting would not be there when he comes in and out. It would be replaced later. We had a kind of diving board with a guy sitting on it; if he's going into it, he's sitting on the board, or if he's coming out of it, then he's reaching out. We then put the painting in later and Pixomondo came up with the cool effects."

ABIGAIL ADAMS

Adams was a tireless detective, the Watson to Katrina Crane's Holmes. While Adams' husband John (who once found Crane in a broom closet, hiding from Betsy Ross) fought for people's rights as a lawyer in public, she fought for the under-represented in private. During one of her investigations, Adams hunted down and stopped the "blood artist" James Colby.

Above: *Actress Michelle Trachtenberg in full costume as Abigail Adams.*

Left and Below: *Digital drawing and painting concepts for the artist's loft set.*

Opposite: *The final dressed set.*

Above: Blueprints for the set and an area of the final dressed set.

Right and Opposite: One of the final Colby prop paintings being painted, and a final painting..

'The stretching out of the painting and how it snaps back is something we researched and developed to know what it would look like. We didn't want it to feel like he's stepping out of a wormhole. We wanted an old-time feel and to make it look less visual-effects driven.'

Jason Michael Zimmerman (VFX Supervisor)

The troubled Carmilla Pines, from Nick Hawley's past, came with the kind of baggage we've come to expect from a newly introduced *Sleepy Hollow* character: she could turn into a monster. However, for costume designer Kristin Burke, the challenges didn't begin with dressing the demonic form, it started with simpler necessities. Footwear. And party dresses. "It was scripted that she has interesting shoes. The third time we see her, she is dressed for a party and needed a beautiful, Indian chemise. That way, when she turned into the vitala, she would look fully realized as a goddess monster," explains Burke. "The beautiful shoes with the gold heels were Yves Saint Laurent. Jaime Murray was cast a week before shooting and we managed to get the only pair in her size."

The color of Carmilla's dress was inspired by Hindu folklore. "The vitala is a very interesting concept – if you do a web search, you'll see all kinds of images of this blue entity," Burke continues.

"There was a lot of talk about doing blue skin, or putting her in something authentically Indian. I ended up having to find five matching turquoise chemises in Wilmington. We found that if we drove to [nearby town] Raleigh, we could get an extra one."

With 6' 6" stunt actor Alexander Ward playing the fully transformed vitala (and Murray being 5' 5"), VFX supervisor Jason Michael Zimmerman came in to enhance makeup department head Corey Castellano's prosthetic work. "In the case of Jaime Murray's character, we made a life-cast," explains Castellano, "and then we had to scan her," adds Zimmerman. "We knew we would have some transformation shots, which is a lot of what we do. We'll usually do the transformation, but the 'before and after' elements are Corey's work. For us, it's about coming up with a cool idea on how to make it happen and not look like a morph. We had a CG version of her in two different stages. A couple times they did it in camera, and the other times VFX did it."

COSTUME DESIGN

Earrings - gold & Dangly

Skull necklace - gold (all Kali have skull necklaces)

Gold-toned indian cuff bracelet

Blue silk jersey - SAME COLOR AS KALI'S SKIN - drapey one shoulder "goddess" dress. Clings to the body. Built-in pushup bra

SLEEPY HOLLOW
EP 214

CARMILLA

Gold strappy shoes - something festive

NICK HAWLEY
'The whole thing about Hawley is that he's a straight-out avatar. We had eight pairs of G-star pants, 12 different Henleys and an awesome leather jacket.'
Kristin M. Burke
(Series Costume Designer)

Above: *The costume design for Carmilla's party dress and shoes.*

Opposite: *Stunt actor Alexander Ward as the vitala.*

Above: *Actor Matt Barr as Nick Hawley in his G-star pants and Henley.*

Mabie's Tavern

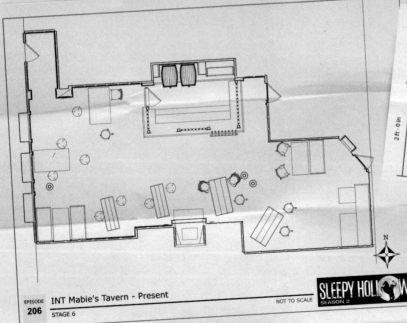

EPISODE **206** · INT Mabie's Tavern - Present · STAGE 6 · NOT TO SCALE

SLEEPY HOLLOW · SEASON 2

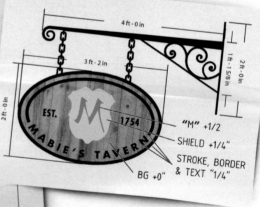

4 ft - 0 in

3 ft - 2 in

1 ft - 15/8 in

2 ft - 0 in

2 ft - 0 in

EST. 1754

M

MABIE'S TAVERN

"M" +1/2

SHIELD +1/4

STROKE, BORDER & TEXT "1/4"

BG +0"

Top: *Concept art for areas of the tavern interior as they appear in 1778 (left) and 2014 (right).*

Left: *Blueprint for the tavern.*

Above: *Concept art for the tavern sign.*

'Mabie's Tavern was modeled on a pub I used to go to in London, so I managed to create my own little London pub here.'

Jeremy Cassells (Season Two Production Designer)

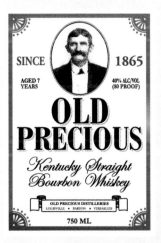

SINCE 1865

AGED 7 YEARS

40% ALC/VOL (80 PROOF)

OLD PRECIOUS

Kentucky Straight Bourbon Whiskey

OLD PRECIOUS DISTILLERIES
LOUISVILLE • BARTON • VERSAILLES

750 ML

Make no mistake our whiskey has the most courage well known for many years as the best that money can buy.

Government Warning

(1) The consumption of alcohol can cause a faint buzz, progressing to a complete passing out. Once on the ground one should be kept facing to the side as to avoid drowning in vomit. (2) Liqueur may make women appear dangerously more attractive than in real life leading to accidental children

0 66483 16687 0

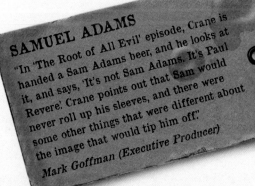

SAMUEL ADAMS

"In 'The Root of All Evil' episode, Crane is handed a Sam Adams beer, and he looks at it, and says, 'It's not Sam Adams. It's Paul Revere.' Crane points out that Sam would never roll up his sleeves, and there were some other things that were different about the image that would tip him off."

Mark Goffman (Executive Producer)

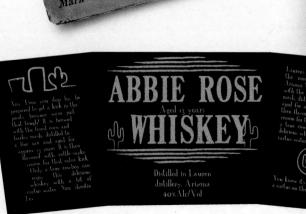

ABBIE ROSE WHISKEY

Aged 13 years

Distilled in Lauren distillery, Arizona

40% Alc/Vol

Solomon Kent

Towards the end of season two, warlock Solomon Kent entered the game of good vs. evil and changed the rules, nudging Katrina Crane towards a dark path of blood magic. Costume designer Kristin Burke had the challenge of coming up with a striking look for the character well before Johnathon Schaech took on the role. "We didn't know who would be cast, so I asked a hat maker to make a hat in its biggest form, because inevitably the actor would have to wear a wig and it would add inches to the circumference of the hat." Burke adds that the character's aesthetic was inspired by a comic book relation to another, all-powerful man: Superman. "There was a lot of back and forth about Solomon Kent, but Silas Kent [a comic-book ancestor to Clark Kent's adoptive parents], had this particular style of hat. Solomon also had that coat with the belt, but the important things for the character were that hat and the stand of the collar."

When it came to the man inside the clothes, makeup department head Corey Castellano's task was two-fold. "We wanted to make sure there was a really big visual juxtaposition between when he was a benevolent village minister, and his transition to an evil warlock. He initially had a very clean and tidy makeup. We got into the slightly more worn look when he starts shedding his own blood for magic. When he's going over to the dark side there's a little bit more beard stubble, his eyes are milkier, and we added sweat, and of course, the scarification. First he only has one or two cuts on his arms. The next time we see him perpetrating evil in modern times, his arms and chest are covered in them. That means you know that he's been up to no good for quite a while."

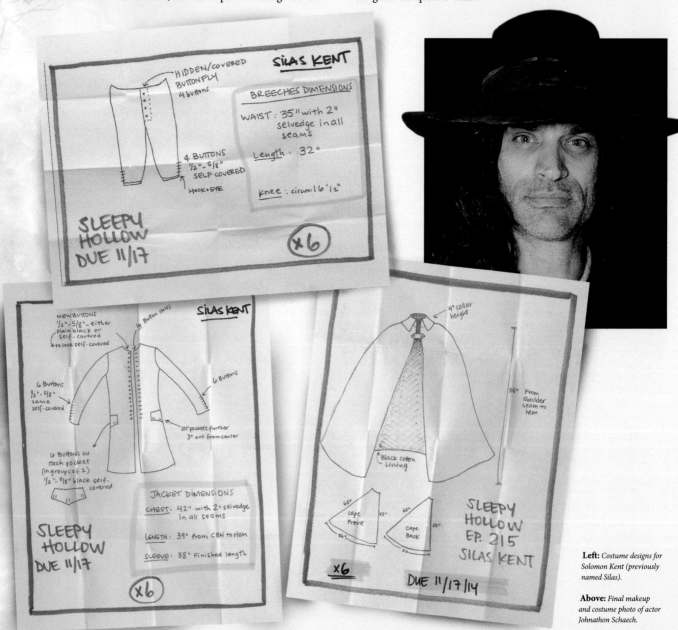

Left: *Costume designs for Solomon Kent (previously named Silas).*

Above: *Final makeup and costume photo of actor Johnathon Schaech.*

ELIZABETHAN
Epoch Collection

ITEM CATALOGUE

Bid on rare and valuable items from
Great Britain's golden age

Above and Right: *The auction house catalogue featuring the "grand grimoire", Kent steals.*

CLARIDGE'S
AUCTION HOUSE

ASSORTED

ANTIQUE LOVESEAT	
Family:	R.S.
Lot. nr:	43A
D.A. nr:	46
Starting Price:	$750

ITEM NAME	
Family:	R.S.
Lot. nr:	42
D.A. nr:	48
Starting Price:	$2500

ITEM NAME	
Family:	R.S.
Lot. nr:	42
D.A. nr:	50
Starting Price:	$4000

Lot. nr:	42B
D.A. nr:	49
Starting Price:	$3100

ITEM NAME	
Family:	R.S.
Lot. nr:	35
D.A. nr:	51
Starting Price:	$220

RED LEATHER SOFA	
Family:	R.S.
Lot. nr:	34
D.A. nr:	52
Starting Price:	$2200

ITEM NAME	
Family:	R.S.
Lot. nr:	34
D.A. nr:	53
Starting Price:	$1800

ITEM NAME	
Family:	R.S.
Lot. nr:	22
D.A. nr:	54
Starting Price:	$3400

FEATURED ITEM

"GRAND GRIMOIRE"	
Family:	P.M.
Lot. nr:	43A
D.A. nr:	55
Starting Price:	$7500

DETAIL

16th Century Bible	
Family:	R.S.
Lot. nr:	42
D.A. nr:	56
Starting Price:	$2200

SHAKESPEARE VOLUME	
Family:	R.S.
Lot. nr:	43A
D.A. nr:	57
Starting Price:	$3200

BERNARDINO LUINI	
Family:	R.S.
Lot. nr:	25A
D.A. nr:	58
Starting Price:	$3500

ENTRY TABLE	
Family:	R.S.
Lot. nr:	26B
D.A. nr:	59
Starting Price:	$21

FOLIO COLLECTION	
Family:	R.S.
Lot. nr:	22A
D.A. nr:	60
Starting Price:	$1500

MARCO BASAITI PAINTING	
Family:	R.S.
Lot. nr:	43B
D.A. nr:	61
Starting Price:	$2900

PIERO DI COSIMO - 14	
Family:	R.S.
Lot. nr:	43B
D.A. nr:	62
Starting Price:	$2100

ANTIQUE LUTE	
Family:	R.S.
Lot. nr:	16
D.A. nr:	63
Starting Price:	$950

Page 6

Page 7

' It was important that Solomon could access his forearm to draw blood. I designed a jacket with ten buttons along the forearm so he easily can do that. It was supposed to be Puritan, so they would not have as many buttons because it was decorative, but for the story, it fit our purpose.'

Kristin Burke (Costume Designer)

Below: *The security camera visual effects sequence in 'Spellcaster.'*

The Village

"We went out to the Roanoke set and looked at it. It had been out in the weather for nearly a year [since episode 105], so we came up with ways of changing the scale so that it became a bigger village for the Kent storyline [episode 215]. The director really wanted to see outside the church, so we decided to do the interior and the exterior in the same place. We then chose our angles so we could actually see the village and dresssed it so the audience wouldn't know it was Roanoke. It was an exercise in expanding on what we already had to give it more scope. That's something that I always try and do, trying to give scale and scope without bending too many historical rules with the time that I have because, in the end, the camera can always be somewhat fooled. Then we also have VFX that can fill in, but nearly all of that set was practical. You add wardrobe, some animals, smoke, some great dialogue, and there you have it."

Jeremy Cassells (Season Two Production Designer)

This Spread: *The Roanoke set from 'John Doe' that was redressed to be the home of Solomon Kent in 'Spellcaster.'*

Jefferson's Fenestella

'We had a brilliant artist in the art department who made a lot of books! She has this copy that you see in one of the flashbacks of Jefferson hand-writing the Declaration of Independence and Crane is commenting on it. It's an edited copy with some strike-outs and other things. It's a really cool visual.'

Mark Goffman (Executive Producer)

Above and Left: *3D renders of the Fenestella set, including period art.*

Below: *A photo of the final set.*

Right: *Actor Steven Weber as Thomas Jefferson.*

THOMAS JEFFERSON

"In the season two finale, at that point in time, Washington and Jefferson really were both in Virginia, and Franklin had just returned from France. We took advantage of that for that story. It's not clear Franklin was in Sleepy Hollow at the time, but as it turns out, he was!"

Mark Gof man (Executive Producer)

'Jeremy Cassells just blew us away with the Fenestella. Towards the end of the season, perhaps your budget is getting squeezed and everyone is getting tired and starting to look towards hiatus... But that's not the way anyone operates on Sleepy Hollow. Every episode becomes something that everybody puts a lot of pride into and does inspired work on, and the Fenestella was one of them. It could have been a very modest space, but not for our Thomas Jefferson! Jeremy and Natalie Weinmann and our production department really blew us away with this truly Jeffersonian architecture to store all of the materials they had gathered for the Witnesses. Then the dome ceiling was a CGI visual effects addition in post-production.'

Mark Goffman (Executive Producer)

Left: *Blueprint of the Fenestella.*

Below: *Interior set photography of the dressed Fenestella.*

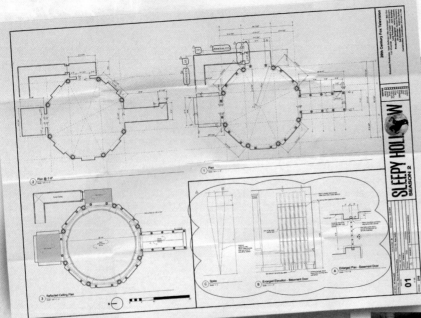

"It was really fun trying to figure out how the Fenestella would work. There are logic things to consider. We worked closely with the writers, trying to figure out a way that the visuals would work. Being a production designer, you've got to try and take a leap of faith with the story, try and embellish the story. If I do my job well, the background is believable and it doesn't distract from the narrative the actors are playing. We did a lot of research on the architecture for it. It was based on a plaza in Spain that I took some things from, but added a twist of fun, not trying to be too slavish to an architectural root."
Jeremy Cassells (Season Two Production Designer)

Above: *The blueprint (left) and an original design sketch (right) for the power chamber prop.*

Below: *Ichabod meets Jefferson in 'What Lies Beneath.'*

The Reavers

When it comes to visceral terror on *Sleepy Hollow*, you'll have trouble finding a monster as physically disturbing as a reaver. Makeup department head Corey Castellano recalls even his fellow crew-members were freaked out by the creations. "I walked onto the set with a bunch of these guys as reavers, and I had people stop and stare as if to say, 'What is wrong with you?!'" he chuckles. "But hey, it's my job. It's fun to push the envelope."

The origin of the Fenestella's twisted protectors is as complex and imaginative as you'd expect from this show. "[Writer] Damian Kindler and I were talking about the reavers having been mercenaries, Celtic warrior-types who went into service. We wanted to do something specific to that period, but then we wanted to make them creepier," reveals Castellano. "I think it was me who initially came up with the idea that these guys have been living in the dark. They're kind of hibernating and subsisting on whatever they could get, but they're magically augmented, as it's been 200 years. There are no females, so they can't breed, but they modified themselves for life in the dark. Len [Wiseman] and I then spitballed a couple of design ideas back and forth. The next thing I knew, I had these guys who had basically peeled their faces back into this really creepy, animalistic, cave-dwelling mode. I would say that's probably the most disturbing thing that I've done, certainly on this show."

Left: *Concept art of a reaver.*

This Page and Next Spread: *Actors in final prosthetics, makeup, and costumes on the Fenestella tunnels set.*

'They split their lips so their teeth are exposed. They peeled their eyelids back so they're geared for the dark. And that dark magic energy from the power source? It helped boost those changes.'

Corey Castellano (Makeup Department Head)

Last Words

During the course of the first two seasons, and 31 hours, the *Sleepy Hollow* creative team has ingeniously woven two hundred years of American history together with the imagined denizens of Purgatory and Hell. The result is a visual feast of endlessly imaginative and surprising environments, characters and creatures.

It's the rare television playground that affords such a fertile expanse for creativity and the show has tellingly attracted a talented community of artists who have left their mark on this re-imagining of Washington Irving's *Sleepy Hollow*. From its inception, the series has been different. Original production designer Alec Hammond perhaps summarizes its uniqueness best, explaining that "*Sleepy Hollow* has a sly commentary and sarcasm. You have a guy come from 1776 who actually knows more about the history and the foundation of the country than the people who live in it. That allows Ichabod, with an 'innocent eye' point of view, to recognize some of the absurdities of our present time, and comment on them. We wanted to do that visually, too."

From the absurd to the terrifying, the historic to the modern, the grotesque to the refined, *Sleepy Hollow* is a show rife with dichotomies. Something that could have led to it being rejected whole-heartedly by a confused audience. Instead, "Sleepyheads" around the globe have embraced its "wild and crazy" philosophy and welcomed audacious creativity to their screens. It's why the show, and the creativity in these pages, exist.

"I'm so grateful to our fan base," co-creator Alex Kurtzman enthuses. "As someone who considers himself somewhat of a fan boy, I think fans are critical of the material they love for very good reasons. It's precious to them, but it's a subgenre that a lot of people don't take seriously and they want it to be taken seriously. We've really listened to the fans online for the past two seasons about the things working and not working. The vision of the show has been developed by the community and it's part of the joy of the show to make it for our fans."

Acknowledgements

The authors of this book would like to thank all of the artisans in the various production departments over the course of two seasons for sharing the personal photos and assets which have made this book so special. And the entire K/O Paperworks team, especially Len Wiseman, Alex Kurtzman, Bob Orci, Mark Goffman, Aaron Baiers, and Kristen Gross.

The department heads would also like to thank their crews in particular:

Leo Corey Castellano, Makeup Department Head
  and Special Makeup Effects Designer
Joe Badiali, Shop Supervisor
Dalton Kutsch, Shop Supervisor
Stephen Imhoff, Shop Coordinator / Lab Technician
Eric Koo, Lead Sculptor
Ernesto Cornejo, Sculptor
Erick Rodriguez, Sculptor
John Wrightson, Sculptor
Christy Alexander, Lab Technician
Scott Fields, Lab Technician
Chase Birdsong, Lab Technician
T.J. Loza, Lab Tech / Runner
Anthony Brooks, Key Makeup
Mark Nieman, Key Special Makeup Effects
Jorie Malan, Makeup and Makeup Effects
Cheyenne Carson, Makeup and Makeup Effects
Jamillah Simmons, Makeup
Ashley Plegger, Makeup

Alec Hammond, Production Designer for the pilot and season 1
Alan Hook, Art Director
Kathy Lucas, Set Decorator
Zachary Fannin, Graphic Designer
Bill Davis, Art Director
Matthew Sullivan, Set Decorator
Brian Baker, Set Designer
Shannon Bourne, Graphic Designer
Mike Hull, Construction Coordinator
Jeremy Cassells, Production Designer for season 2
Natalie Weinmann, Art Director
Shannon Bourne, Assistant Art Director
Ryan Garton, Set Designer
Barbara E. Harris, Art Department Coordinator
Paul Markovich, Graphic Designer
Lee Bailey, Art Department PA
Adam Cameron, Leadman
Rachel Wilkin, Buyer
Beth Bromley, Buyer
Joseph R. McGuire Jr., Charge Hand
Michael Marcelli, Charge Hand

Scott Blackmon, Set Dresser
Duane Williamson, Set Dresser
Billy Alford, Set Dresser
Eric Skipper, Set Dresser
Steven R. Hawk, Set Dresser
Blake Hartley, Set Dresser
Matt Collins, Set Dresser
Travis Sullivan, Set Dresser
Vince Immordino, On Set Dresser

Tyler Patton, Property Master
John Bankson, Property Master
Guillaume DeLouche, Property Master

Sanja Milkovic Hays, Costume Designer for pilot and season 1
Nava R. Sadan, Costume Supervisor
Irena Stepic-Rendulic
Christian Cordella
Serzhik Kazarian
Francine Lecoultre
Julia Rusthoven, Set Costumer
Jeanie Baker, Set Costumer
Kristin M. Burke, Costume Designer for seasons 1 and 2
Mairi Chisholm, Costume Designer for end of season 2
Tiger Curran, Assistant Costume Designer
Erin Lambert, Key / Truck Costumer
Janet Marie Ross, Set Costumer
Jason Blackan, Costumer
Darek Beeman, Tailor
Melissa Binder, Ager / Dyer
Kelly Errigo Mason, Costumer
Julie Love, Costumes PA
Blake Blackman, Costumes PA

Jason Zimmerman, Visual Effects Supervisor
Eddie Bonin, VFX Producer
Ante Dekovic, VFX Plate Supervisor
Aleksandra Kochoska, VFX Data Wrangler
And all of the visual effects company vendors, including
  Pixomondo, Synaptic VFX, Origin Digital Studios,
  Basilic Fly Studio, BOT VFX, FuseFX and Zoic Studios.